2 Corinthians
Personal Workbook

By Chad Sychtysz

© 2024 Spiritbuilding Publishers.
All rights reserved. No part of this book may be reproduced in any form without the written permission of the publisher.

Published by
Spiritbuilding Publishers
9700 Ferry Road, Waynesville, Ohio 45068

2 CORINTHIANS PERSONAL WORKBOOK
By Chad Sychtysz

ISBN: 978-1955285-99-5

Spiritbuilding
PUBLISHERS

spiritbuilding.com

Table of Contents

Introduction to *2 Corinthians* 1

SECTION ONE: Paul's Physical and Spiritual Ministry (1:3—7:16) 5

Salutation (1:1-2) 5

Lesson 1: Paul's Comfort and Confidence (1:3-22) 5

Lesson 2: The Reason for Paul's Writing (1:23—2:17) 10

Lesson 3: Ministers of a New Covenant (3:1-18) 14

Lesson 4: The Sacrificial Nature of Paul's Ministry (4:1-18) 18

Lesson 5: Our Future Glory through the Ministry of Reconciliation (5:1-21) ... 25

Lesson 6: The Genuineness of Paul's Ministry (6:1—7:1) 33

Lesson 7: Paul's Appeal for the Corinthians' Affection (7:2-16) 43

SECTION TWO: Monetary Collection and Principles of Giving (8:1—9:15) 47

Lesson 8: Paul Reminds the Corinthians of Their Pledge (8:1-24) 47

Lesson 9: Principles of Charitable Contributions (9:1-15) 52

SECTION THREE: Paul's Defense of His Apostleship (10:1—13:10) 57

Lesson 10: Paul's Response to His Accusers 57

Lesson 11: Paul's Challenge to His Accusers 63

Lesson 12: Visions and a "Thorn" (12:1-13) 73

Lesson 13: Final Admonitions (12:14—13:10) 73

Final Commendations and Closing Thoughts (13:11-14) 83

Sources Used for This Study 85

Endnotes 87

Introduction to 2 *Corinthians*

*S*econd *Corinthians* is not one of the popular books of the New Testament (NT). Its theme, content, format, and emphasis are altogether different from *1 Corinthians*, and thus it does not appear to serve as a nice, neat sequel. The apostle Paul's writing style is often more expressive (versus intellectual), making it difficult to read. "Its language is loose, cumbersome, and marked by sudden breaks; there are digressions and parenthetical asides throughout the letter."[1] "It is the least systematic of all his writings and is filled with emotion."[2] For these reasons, it lies in the shadow of its far more practical sister epistle and is perhaps one of the least appreciated of Paul's epistles.

What the second letter to the Corinthians *does* offer, however, is perhaps the most revealing look into the apostle Paul himself, as well as his disposition toward the work and struggles of a true apostle of Christ. It is more personally insightful and poignant ("a tumult of contending emotions"[3]) than any of his other extant writings; in it, "Paul bares his heart and his life as he does in none of his other letters."[4] *Second Corinthians* provides several facets of Paul's ministry that Acts does not. It also reveals a lot about his devotion to the Corinthians themselves, much more than is revealed in either *Acts* or *1 Corinthians*.

The City of Corinth: Corinth ["ornament"] was an important commercial city of ancient Greece, being ideally situated on the western end of the isthmus between the Peloponnesian peninsula and the European mainland. It was strategically positioned at the intersection of north-south land trade routes *and* east-west sea trade routes, providing safe passage between the Aegean and Adriatic Seas.[5]

Corinth's beginnings date as far back as the 7th century BC. During most of the 3rd and 4th centuries BC, it remained under Macedonian control. In 196 BC, the city was given limited autonomy by Rome, but it rebelled against Roman rule only fifty years later. As a result of

this, Rome thoroughly destroyed the city (146 BC), and it became a sparsely populated ruin for one hundred years. In 46 BC, Julius Caesar declared Corinth a Roman colony, rebuilt the city, it rapidly regained its prominence as well as unprecedented prosperity.[6] Unfortunately, its paganism, hedonism, and wickedness also flourished; the term "Corinthian" became synonymous with gross immorality in the Mediterranean world. The city was also steeped in idolatry and temple prostitution: Apollo, Poseidon, Athena, and Aphrodite were among some of the principal gods worshiped there.[7]

Author and Date of Writing: There is little dispute over the authorship of *2 Corinthians*. The apostle Paul is undoubtedly the genuine author of this work. Both the internal and external evidence, especially when corroborating with what is recorded in *Acts*, overwhelmingly points to this. Paul first visited Corinth on his second missionary journey (Acts 18:1ff), circa AD 51 or 52, a visit which followed a relatively poor reception of the gospel in Athens (Acts 17:16ff). He established a church in Corinth and remained there for eighteen months (Acts 18:11). Re-educating the worldly, sensual-minded Corinthians to think and act like Christians was a difficult process; even after all of Paul's instruction, the Corinthians continued to grapple with their deeply imbedded paganism.

What we call "First Corinthians" was in response to problems that Paul had heard were going on in the church in Corinth. (In fact, Paul had already written the Corinthians once before—a letter that has since been lost to history; see 1 Cor. 5:9.) After writing *1 Corinthians*, Paul's earnest intention was to revisit Corinth, but he sent Timothy and Erastus to them first (Acts 19:22, 1 Cor. 16:5–11), and Titus. Paul waited anxiously for word from Titus as to how this letter had been received (2 Cor. 2:12–13), since it dealt with several difficult topics and required Paul to be rather forceful in some of his comments. After an agonizing delay, Paul finally learned that the Corinthians (in general) had received his letter in the spirit in which it had been written and had repented of their sins (2 Cor. 7:6–9). There remained, however, a group of "false apostles" who challenged Paul's apostolic authority (2 Cor. 11:12–13), and Paul's response to these men is largely the subject of *2 Corinthians*. It appears that Paul did not actually visit Corinth again until after the writing of this second epistle.

Second Corinthians was written from Macedonia (possibly Philippi), ca. AD 56–57, while Paul was on what is known as his third missionary journey (Acts 18:23—21:17). Paul wrote it in preparation for his intended visit to Corinth (2 Cor. 12:14, 13:1), to smooth out the relationship between himself and the church there; bring closure to some of their past struggles; and instruct them regarding the collection being gathered for the saints in need in Jerusalem.

Purpose and Theme: The overall occasion for this letter concerns the strained relationship between the Corinthians and Paul.[8] Two major reasons existed for this. First, there was the issue of the "immoral man" (1 Cor. 5) whose situation created a great deal of unnecessary tension between Paul and the Corinthians. Second, there were rebels within the Corinthian church ("a dangerous and defiant minority"[9]) who still resisted Paul's authority. These men were likely Jews who themselves were being externally influenced by Jews elsewhere (as in Acts 15:1).[10] They claimed to know more about the gospel than did Paul, and they ridiculed his personal integrity and authority. Some of their accusations against him included cowardice, vacillation, personal insecurity, fiery talk with no substance, no letters of commendation (i.e., from Jerusalem), doubts about his knowledge of the Law (of Moses), insinuations about his honesty, and charges of self-ambition and profiteering.

Paul was both heartbroken and insulted over this. At the time of the writing of *2 Corinthians*, he was in the process of collecting money from predominantly Gentile churches in Macedonia and Achaia (Greece) to give to the predominantly Jewish churches in Judea as a relief effort for the famine there. Paul's opponents ("most eminent apostles," as he sarcastically refers to them—11:5) claimed that he was collecting money for himself and had "deceived" the Corinthians by using other men (such as Titus) to make it appear that he was not involved. Paul's intention, then, is to set the record straight and to prove his sincerity in all he did for the Corinthians.

Second Corinthians' design is not as well structured as we see in other letters, simply because of its highly emotional and personal content. The first nine chapters (1—9) indicate a kind of reconciliation between Paul and the Corinthians—at least, the Corinthians that respected, trusted, and listened to him. The remainder of the epistle (chapters 10—13) carries a very different tone and is pointedly directed at those within the Corinthian church who are causing friction, undermining Paul's credibility, and gloating over their own knowledge and status.

While not an in-depth doctrinal treatise (as, say, *Romans*), *2 Corinthians* does offer some theological teachings that are expounded upon nowhere else in the NT. These include certain teachings on the "new covenant" (2:12—4:16); our earthly dwelling and heavenly "clothing" (4:7—5:10); and the "ministry of reconciliation" (5:11-21). Paul also offers revealing insight to the difficult ministry which Christ required of him (2 Cor. 11:22-33; see Acts 9:15-16) and provides the characteristics of a "true apostle" (2 Cor. 12:12).

General Outline

- **Salutation (1:1-2)**
- **Section One: Paul's Physical and Spiritual Ministry (1:3—7:16)**
  - Paul's Comfort and Confidence (1:3-22)
  - The Reason for Paul's Writing (1:23—2:17)
  - Ministers of a New Covenant (3:1-18)
  - The Sacrificial Nature of Paul's Ministry (4:1-18)
  - Our Future Glory through the Ministry of Reconciliation (5:1-21)
  - The Genuineness of Paul's Ministry (6:1—7:1)
  - Paul's Appeal for the Corinthians' Affections (7:2-16)
- **Section Two: Monetary Collection and Principles of Giving (8:1—9:15)**
  - Paul Reminds the Corinthians of Their Pledge (8:1-24)
  - Principles of Charitable Contributions (9:1-15)
- **Section Three: Paul's Defense of His Apostleship (10:1—13:10)**
- **Paul's Response to His Accusers (10:1-18)**
  - Paul's Challenge to His Accusers (11:1-33)
  - Visions and a "Thorn" (12:1-13)
  - Final Admonitions (12:14—13:10)
- **Final Commendations and Closing Thoughts (13:11-14)**

Salutation (1:1–2)

"Paul, an apostle of Christ Jesus by the will of God" (1:1)—a necessary introduction for a church wrestling with compliance to apostolic authority (see 1 Cor 1:1). In other words: Paul reasserts himself as an *apostle* of God writing to the "*church* of God" at Corinth. Despite the mention of Timothy, this entire letter is in Paul's voice, with his words, and by his apostolic authority.

Both the apostle and the saints [lit., holy ones] belong to and derive their approval from "God our Father and the Lord Jesus Christ." This immediately establishes the context of the letter: God commissioned Paul to instruct His saints, and He expects His saints to listen to that instruction. "Achaia" likely refers to the entire peninsula south of Macedonia, of which Corinth was the capital.[11]

SECTION ONE: PAUL'S PHYSICAL AND SPIRITUAL MINISTRY (1:3—7:16)

Lesson One:
Paul's Comfort and Confidence (1:3–22)

The God of All Comfort (1:1–7): Mercy and comfort (1:3) are major themes of this letter, concepts which resonate throughout it in the form of "reconciliation," "grace," "life," "glory," "joy," etc. "Mercy" is the sparing of a deserved punishment; it is often synonymous with "compassion." "Comfort" means "to strengthen (through the encouragement of another)."[12] Paul recognized God as the original *source* of all mercy and comfort; there is no divine comfort outside of a right relationship with Him. As God comforts one member of the body, so that comfort can extend to others (1:4).

One cannot receive genuine comfort without first having genuinely suffered; the more intense the suffering, the sweeter and more appreciated God's comfort will be (1:5). The specific comfort to which Paul refers is the favorable report from Titus concerning how the Corinthians had received his previous letter (2 Cor. 7:6–7, 13). Paul had written to them strongly and feared that they might not respond appropriately to what he had said. His intention was not merely to expose their errors, but to have them repent of their sins (2 Cor. 7:8–9).

Paul does not keep his joy of divine comfort to himself, however. He speaks freely of the "sufferings" that he (and others) has endured for the sake of the gospel (1:6–7). He sees a direct correlation between what has happened to him personally and what will profit the church in Corinth. Paul is not saying that his comfort could save anyone, but that mercy, comfort, and compassion are instrumental in and contribute toward one's salvation. Whatever he has learned and gained through God's having comforted him is to the Corinthians' spiritual advantage.

Real Suffering, Real Comfort (1:8–11): Paul is not speaking only in theoretical or abstract terms, however, when he talks about suffering. He is not giving them a sermon on "suffering" but is alluding to real-world and painful experiences that he has endured (1:8). His reference to his "affliction…in Asia" may allude to a specific event (Acts 19:23–41) or the general trouble he faced in the Roman province of Asia Minor (see 1 Cor. 15:32, a figurative expression).

"Trust" and "deliverance" (1:9–10) are positive themes which accompany the concepts of suffering and comfort. One's perilous physical, mental, or emotional situation ought to increase his dependence upon the soul-strengthening support that God alone can provide (Eph. 3:16–17). The "sentence of death" (later expounded upon in 2 Cor. 4:11–12) refers to the ever-present danger that Paul and his co-workers faced in preaching the gospel of Christ. This danger is due to: preaching to a hostile audience (specifically, unbelieving Jews); enemies within the brotherhood (who wanted Paul to fail so they might be justified); and the rigors of travel in the ancient world (robbers, bandits, storms at sea, wild animals, etc.). Just as God "raises the dead" (1:9; see Heb. 11:19), so He can raise the hopes of those whose circumstances seem hopeless (Rom. 4:18–21). "When the need is greatest, God is nearest."[13] Paul faced peril and death on several occasions (as he later describes in 2 Cor. 11), yet always kept his faith in the Great Deliverer. His hope was not in man-made deliverance, or even in his self-resourcefulness, but in divine providence (1:10).[14] He also believed in the power of prayer, and especially the power of the *collective* prayers of God's people (1:11).

Confidence and Commitment (1:12–22): "Confidence" (1:12) is another theme that repeatedly resurfaces throughout this epistle. Paul expresses his confidence in the way he and fellow ministers have conducted themselves ("in holiness and godly sincerity"[15]); the Corinthians themselves (2 Cor. 7:4, 16); and his being able to visit them soon if all goes according to plan (1:15). Nonetheless, Paul realizes that the saints in Corinth may not have fully understood all he had written earlier (1:13–14); in fact, some of Paul's writings are difficult for anyone to grasp (2 Pet. 3:16). Even so, the *intention* of his writing was so that they (and we) *could* read and *could* understand (see Eph. 3:4). He implies here that whatever he wrote earlier *had not changed*, and therefore he had no reason to retract any of it, but only to provide more clarity to it.[16]

Paul also implies that he had been prevented from visiting them earlier, or that he had visited them only very briefly, and not as long as he had hoped (1:15–16). Regardless, he assures the Corinthians that he has not deceived them by failing to do what he had promised (1:17).[17] He is not making plans that only suit his own interests (i.e., "according to the flesh"); he has the concerns of the entire brotherhood weighing heavily upon him always (2 Cor. 11:28). Thus, "our word to you is not yes and no" (1:18)—he is not telling them one thing but doing the opposite. The gospel of Christ— just like God Himself—is not a contradictory message, nor should be the promises of those who preach that gospel. "God is faithful" (see also 1 Cor. 1:9 and 10:13) means that He does not talk out of both sides of His mouth, but whatever He promises, He is certain to fulfill.

Paul is not saying, "I am as faithful to you as God is," for Paul is only a man, even though he is a servant of the Lord. Circumstances beyond his control could delay him (e.g., 1 Thess. 2:18), but nothing can delay God. Even so, Paul is affirming the sincerity of his own personal promise to the Corinthians. Just as Christ is God's "Amen" [lit., truly; yes; so be it] to believers, Paul is Christ's "yes" to the church at Corinth (1:19–20). Christ is the One who *fulfills* the promises of God; "the eternal purpose" of God was "carried out in Christ Jesus our Lord" (Eph. 3:11).

God the "Father of mercies" (recall 1:3) is also the One who "establishes [or, confirms]," "anointed,"[18] and "sealed" those who belong to Him (1:21–22). These are all divine actions; we initiate them through our faith, and we participate in them as believers, but it is God alone who carries them out.[19] We are not bound to God merely by His desire to save us and our desperate need to be saved. Rather, God secures our relationship with Him with a legally-binding covenant—one sealed by none other than Himself.

To be "sealed" indicates an authoritative stamp of approval, indicating authenticity and ownership (Eph. 1:13–14, 2 Tim. 2:19). The wording here alludes to (but is not *reduced* to) a business transaction, which would be well-understood in the commercial trading world of Corinth.[20] Since we have the "pledge [lit., earnest; down payment[21]]" of His Spirit, we are guaranteed the *full* realization of His promise in time *if* we continue in faith *and* remain faithful till death (Col. 1:23, Rev. 2:10).

Questions

1.) In discussing God's "comfort" (1:3–5), is Paul referring to a miraculous experience or something of a practical nature—as in, something we can receive today?

   a. Or is God's "comfort" (or "mercy") extended only in the form of sparing us from eternal punishment?

   b. Can those who are not "in Christ" experience God's mercy in the same way that Paul speaks of it here? Why or why not?

2.) When a Christian chooses to suffer or rejoice only in private, how does this undermine the instructions of the gospel? What are the benefits of our shared positive *and* negative experiences (see 1 Cor. 12:26, Gal. 6:6, and 1 Pet. 5:9, for example)?

3.) Is God's deliverance from the trials we must face in our walk with Him conditional or unconditional? In other words, in expecting *Him* to perform in this way, is there anything required of *us*?

4.) Paul claims that "God is faithful" (1:18). But to *what* is He faithful? To *whom* is he faithful? Under what circumstances? What if He was *not* faithful?

Lesson Two: The Reason for Paul's Writing (1:23—2:17)

Paul now reveals (1:23–24) that there was more to the delay of his visit than whatever was detaining him.[22] He purposely "did not come again" right away in order to "spare" the Corinthians (by giving them time to repent), not because he was trying to avoid them (1:23–24). He did not want to come to them in an imposing way, but as fellow "workers with you for your joy." He thought that coming to them earlier would have undermined that objective. He did not want another "sorrowful [or, painful]" visit, implying that there had already *been* one.[23]

A Successful Disciplinary Action (2:4–11): Many scholars and commentators believe that Paul had what has been dubbed an "intermediate journey" to Corinth between the time he wrote *1 Corinthians* from Ephesus and the writing of this epistle (Acts 20:2). This is the "sorrowful" visit (implied in 2:1–4) which allegedly prompted a letter (which, if indeed it once did exist, no longer does). This would also explain the "third time" he would come to them (12:14, 13:1). Because of this sorrowful visit, the relationship between the Corinthians and Paul deteriorated considerably. Paul speaks of "sorrow from those who ought to make me rejoice" (2:3) and "much affliction and anguish of heart" (2:4) that he experienced because of it. He wanted to avoid a repeat of this. Instead, he desired to show his *love* for them.

Without mentioning names or details, Paul now refers to a disciplinary incident within the church at Corinth—an action which he had initiated against a certain brother (2:5–11). Many believe this person to be the one mentioned in 1 Cor. 5—the man who had his "father's wife."[24] In that case, Paul used his apostolic authority to demand that the Corinthians withdraw their fellowship from this man (1 Cor. 5:13). The purpose of that decision was twofold: first, to compel him to repent; second, to "test" the response of the Corinthian church regarding apostolic instruction (see 2:9). The "majority" of the church apparently responded well (2:6), although it may be assumed that some: remained indifferent; sympathized with the man and thus did not end their personal fellowship with him; openly resisted Paul's authority (to be dealt with later).[25] It is possible, too, that some believed the man deserved even more punishment.

In Paul's view, however, the congregational action fulfilled the intended objective; the case against this man is now closed. It is now time to "reaffirm your love for him" (2:8) since the brother has shown "excessive sorrow." In other words, the man repented of his sin and sought God's forgiveness as well as that of the congregation. This calls for a different course of action on the part of the congregation, namely, to forgive this brother and receive him back in full fellowship (2:10). Paul approves of both positive actions: the putting *out* as well as the taking *back*. If they have forgiven him as a godly response toward this man's penitence, then certainly Paul also has forgiven him. He is not going to stand in the way of appropriate Christian action.

To refuse to forgive (when the offending party has met the conditions *for* forgiveness) is to succumb to Satan's "schemes," since Christians are supposed to be a forgiving people (2:11; see Eph. 4:32). Satan's malicious efforts are at the heart of every struggle against sin; the division of fellowship is one of his many devices. Satan did not seek only the brother who had sinned, but also sought to ruin, if possible, the entire congregation.[26] If the congregation withheld its forgiveness and fellowship for vindictive (or other) reasons, this would serve Satan's interests, not God's. However, having dealt correctly with this sin (instead of "arrogantly" as before; see 1 Cor. 5:1–2), Paul was pleased with the Corinthians' response, if only they would now reinstate the penitent brother's fellowship.

Paul's Relief over Titus' News (2:12–17): Paul's original plan was apparently to leave Ephesus for Troas. There he would meet up with his co-worker, Titus, who was supposed to bring him news of how the Corinthians were doing and their regard for his authority. Titus did not come to Troas, however, and Paul himself was preoccupied, taking advantage of the "open door" of opportunity God had provided for him there (2:12). Titus' delay caused Paul all kinds of anxiety, but he had work to carry out among the churches in Macedonia (2:13). It was there that Titus found him and gave him favorable news of the church at Corinth (2:14, implied). Paul's elation and relief are very evident in this passage, and he characterizes the changed attitudes of the church in Corinth as a "triumph."

Paul's "fragrance" reference ("an aroma from death to death" for one person and "life to life" for another) likely alludes to a well-known military procedure in the ancient world (2:15–16a). A victorious general, upon entering his own city, would be saluted with a procession marked with celebration and the burning of spices and incense. This was the fragrance of victory and success. His prisoners of war who followed in the march, however, would smell the same incense and know that death was near, as it was customary to execute captives as a symbol of the conquest of their people. This is the traditional and most natural explanation of this passage.[27]

"Who is adequate for these things?" (2:16b)—i.e., Paul and his fellow apostles recognize that they are not "adequate" to preach this knowledge/"fragrance" on their own merit but have been commissioned by Christ for this very purpose. Thus, "we are not like" the opportunists who see financial or personal gain in the preaching of the gospel (2:17). "The figure here is originally that of a tavern-keeper who mixes poor wine with good to increase his profits."[28] In sharp contrast, Paul preached with the sincerest of motives (see 1 Thess. 2:1–6), and with all accuracy sought to represent Christ and His message.

Questions

1.) Paul grieved over what he had to say to the Corinthians (2:4), yet it was necessary that such words be said. This is often characterized today as "tough love"

   a. Under what general circumstances is tough love the best course of action?

   b. When does tough love cease to be "love" and comes across only as "tough"?

2.) Ideally, the goal of all corrective or punitive discipline is *restoration* (Mat. 18:15–17, Gal. 6:1–2, Heb. 12:10–11, etc.). How does 2:5–8 bear this out so well?

   a. Yet, how can "church discipline" be misunderstood by the congregation that is supposed to administer it—and what is the negative result when it is?

   b. How is the congregation supposed to respond to the repentance of one whom they had previously disciplined?

3.) What "advantage" does Satan seek to gain from Christians, especially in the matter of church discipline (2:11)? How can we avoid being "ignorant of his schemes"?

4.) Paul says, in essence, that Christ's gospel is the source of spiritual *life* as well as the pronouncement of spiritual *death* (2:15–16). What is meant by this? Is it just as important to speak of the negative results of rejecting Christ's gospel as it is to highlight the positive results of obedience to it?

Lesson Three: Ministers of a New Covenant (3:1–18)

The Letter of Believers (3:1–6): In the ancient world, "letters of commendation" (3:1) might accompany a messenger to attest to the genuineness and accuracy of the message itself (as in Rom. 16:1–2). Paul implies here that certain Jews within the church in Corinth doubted his authenticity because he did not have official endorsements from Jerusalem to authorize him to preach the gospel. Thus, he facetiously proposes a ridiculous scenario: that he (the teacher) should be validated as God's messenger by letters of commendation from the Corinthians (the students)! The Corinthians themselves were his "letter" (3:2): the fact that men and women of one of the most pagan societies in the world have been transformed into Christian believers vividly indicates "the Spirit of the living God" is working in them (3:3).

Paul did not write this figurative "letter" but is most certainly instrumental in its having been produced, since he is their "father through the gospel" (1 Cor 4:15). It is true, however, that this "letter" was being "read by all men"—in other words, the transformation happening among the Corinthians is visibly apparent to all who knew of them. This "letter" is written on "human hearts [or, hearts of flesh]" (3:3), thus producing *spiritual* transformation and *genuine* change. Not only this, but Paul is confident this will *always* be the case among those who submit their will to God through Christ (3:4).

Paul is not "adequate" to participate in the proclamation of the gospel on his own merit (3:5). Instead, he gives all credit to God for having so prepared him for this great privilege. Paul then uses this "letter of commendation" concept to comment on a superior "letter" that God Himself writes: His covenant of salvation with men (3:5–6), penned by His Holy Spirit and brought to life by the blood of Christ (Heb. 13:20–21). This "new covenant" supersedes God's previous covenant with Israel (Heb. 8:7–13) since Christ has fulfilled the first covenant (compare Mat. 5:17 and Luke 24:44–48).[29]

The Ministry of Righteousness (3:7–11): While teachers of Judaism put their confidence in "letters carved on stones" (a reference to the inscription of the Ten Commandments on tablets of stone; see Exod. 34:1–28), Paul put his confidence in the life-giving message of the Spirit (3:7). The Jews sought justification through the keeping of laws rather than seeking genuine spiritual change by submitting to God's Spirit (Acts 7:51–53, Rom. 10:2–4). Yet, letters written on stone cannot do what letters written on the human heart can do. "[T]he letter kills, but the Spirit gives life" means: the "letter" of the law only tells a person what is right or wrong. It cannot *justify* or *heal* the wrongdoer but can only condemn him. In contrast, the "letter" written on the human heart provides divine mercy, grace, forgiveness, and true spiritual renewal—things that law *by itself* could never do once a person has violated it in any way (Jas. 2:10). This spiritual "letter" is the new covenant between God and the faithful believer, which is made possible through Christ's own sacrifice on the cross (Mat. 26:28, Luke 22:20). Paul is proud, then, to be a servant (or minister) of this new covenant.

This is not to say, however, that the first covenant was without glory—or that it was ineffective (3:7–11; see Rom. 7:7–12). Indeed, the radiance of Moses' face when he talked with God (Exod. 34:29–35) symbolized the glory of the covenant which he communicated to Israel. Even so, Moses' glory was "fading" in the sense that it was not meant to last, and that Moses himself was not the one who deserved the ultimate glory (cf. Mat. 17:1–5). God's covenant with Israel was "weak" in comparison to the new covenant we have in Christ in that it (the old covenant) could not overcome the insuperable problem of sin. Instead, it sought its fulfillment outside of itself, in Christ (Acts 13:38–39). This "ministry of condemnation" could identify the sinner but could not redeem him of his sin. It "kills" him in the sense that it sentences the sinner to death.

The Lifting of the Veil (3:12–18): The first covenant, gloried as it was, nonetheless resulted in death (condemnation); the second covenant, bursting with a far superior glory, redeems the soul and gives life—and "abundantly" (John 10:10). For this reason, "we use great boldness in our speech" (3:12), where "boldness" refers to confidence, plainness, and openness—i.e., no need for a veil or any such covering. In a further comparison (3:12–15): Moses saw the glory of God, but no one else did;

even his own face, though shining as a result of standing in God's presence, was veiled when he appeared before the Israelites.[30] Paul compares that veil metaphorically to the shroud (or, covering) over the hearts of the Jews who still cling to Moses; "a veil lies over their heart" because they refuse to accept the superiority of Christ. The Jews give unfading allegiance to Moses, not willing to realize that Moses pointed forward to Christ (Deut. 18:15–19, John 5:45–47). Their prejudice against Christ prevents them from seeing Him in the reading of the Law.

Yet, "whenever a man turns to the Lord, the veil is taken away" (3:16)[31] as when Moses' veil was removed when he spoke in God's presence. Similarly, the Christian speaks to God "with unveiled face" (3:18), seeing (by faith—2 Cor. 5:7) the glory of Christ. The antecedent (or, identified subject to which "the Lord" refers) in 3:16–17 is Christ (from 3:14). Paul seems to mean: the Lord *Jesus Christ* is "the Spirit" to which he referred earlier, and that if one should "see" Him in all the figures, types, and prophecies concerning Him in the OT, then all becomes clear.[32] One is thus freed from the veil and freed from his sins (in his obedience to Christ). Thus, from "glory to glory" (3:18)—from one level or degree of glory to the next, just as a child becomes a man (1 Cor. 13:11–12)—the believer ascends in his understanding and observation of the light, image, and majesty of Christ.

Through this discourse, Paul clarifies that he is not yet another minister of an ancient message (the Law of Moses) that was limited in what it was able to accomplish. Instead, he is an apostle (i.e., a sent messenger) of a living message entrusted to him by a Living Spirit, and thus his intention is to communicate *life* and *hope* to the Corinthians, not *death* and *discipline*. The crescendo of this thought is in the transforming power of the covenant of life: we do not merely become servants of God because of this covenant, but we are transformed into something *new* (a thought to which Paul returns in 2 Cor. 5:17).

Because of this transformation, we can look with hope into the eternal realms, since we have a "pledge" of good things to come (recall 1:22; see 4:16–18 and 5:5). This theme reverberates throughout the next two chapters, as we will see.

Questions

1.) Are you a "letter" (3:2–3) that can be read by other people (Christians or not)? If so, what does this mean? What responsibility do you have in this?

2.) How can a "ministry of death" (3:7) still be regarded "with glory"? What is the "death" part of this ministry (of the Law)? What is the "glory" part?

3.) Paul regarded himself and his fellow laborers in the gospel as "servants of a new covenant" (3:6). Are all Christians in a covenant relationship with God? If so, what does this mean, exactly? If not, then to what did we agree when we were baptized into Christ?

4.) Given what Paul says in 3:15–16, what kind of "veil" might lie over the heart of one who claims to be a Christian but does not accept the gospel's teaching? Can a "veil" lay over the heart of one who genuinely *became* a Christian?

Lesson Four:
The Sacrificial Nature of Paul's Ministry
(4:1–18)

The Manifestation of Truth (4:1–2): This chapter opens with Paul having something to say about four different people (4:1–4): first, about himself; second, about his opponents; third, about those who refuse to accept the gospel; and fourth, about Jesus Christ.[33] Given the divine source and life-giving effect of this "new covenant" (the gospel of grace), Paul says confidently, "Therefore, since we have this ministry, we do not lose heart [or, we faint not]" (4:1). He has been entrusted with a great responsibility, but he has kept himself fit for the task. This is in sharp contrast to the message (or preaching) of those who "[walk] in craftiness" or who are "adulterating the word of God" (4:2)—a reference to Judaizers specifically, but also generally to anyone who changes the message (Gal. 1:8, Phil. 3:2–3, 2 Pet. 2:1–3, etc.).

The gospel—as well as the *Christ* of the gospel—is all about light, illumination, openness, and transparency. It has nothing to hide, but it also exposes the deeds of darkness for what they really are—works of Satan (Eph. 5:7–13). Every person whose heart is seeking the truth will also "commend" (or, approve of) those who speak it—whether this be Paul or anyone else who labors in the spreading of the gospel. "[I]n the sight of God" means there is no reason to be ashamed of preaching the truth *or* receiving it.

Blinded by Satan's Influence (4:3–6): Paul calls the gospel of Christ "our gospel" because it is what he preached and is what the Corinthians also believed (4:3; see 1 Cor. 15:1–2). This gospel—a message radiating with heavenly light—is nonetheless unseen, unappreciated, and poorly appraised (1 Cor. 2:14) by those who remain "veiled" to its power. This refers specifically to the Jews of Paul's day who still cling to Moses (John 8:21–24), but also to everyone else since then who rejects it.[34] Such people are "perishing," meaning, they are (spiritually) dead even while they live. Even worse, they are often oblivious to this deadness, being entirely insensitive to God's offer of grace and salvation (1 Cor. 1:18).

While Moses veiled his face because of God's glory, Satan's wicked influence veils the godless world. He is indeed the "god of this world [or, age]" (4:4a; see Eph. 2:1–2), which means that he has seduced many, many people into giving him, even unwittingly, their allegiance.[35] Satan cannot diminish the glory *of* the gospel, but he can blind people *to* its glory. He does not blind their eyes but their *minds*, indicating a deluding, bewitching, or poisoning of their thinking process to regard the truth to be a lie and lies to be true (2 Thess. 2:10–12).[36]

Even so, Satan cannot blind anyone who does not first give him permission to do so. In other words, they blinded *themselves* by allowing Satan to have control over them. God wants people saved (1 Tim 2:4); Satan wants people to be deceived and ruined. God is light, love, life, and knowledge; Satan is filled with darkness, hatred, deception, and death. Each person makes his own decision as to which "light" he will embrace—the true light of God, or the "angel of light" that Satan pretends to be (2 Cor. 11:14). "Blindness of heart is both a sin and a punishment of sin."[37]

Summary of the Veil Analogy

Moses' literal veil (3:7):	shielded the Israelites from seeing the fading glory of his being in God's presence;	indicates the divine source of the Law, but also its limitations (in the "fading").
The (figurative) veil over the hearts of the Jews (3:14–15):	self-inflicted; perpetuated by a lack of faith and understanding;	prevented them from seeing Christ as the fulfillment of God's covenant with Israel.
The (figurative) veil over the hearts of the unconverted (4:3–4):	self-inflicted, but directly influenced by Satan's influence and activity;	describes the blinding effect of the godless world upon those who resist the truth.
The veil is removed (3:14):	the believer "sees" the Father through the redemptive work of the Son of God *and* the ministry of the Spirit of God;	we can look upon the "face of Christ" (in faith), in anticipation of future glory (when we literally behold Him).

The gospel of Christ radiates with the *glory* of Christ—His beauty, majesty, purity, and authority (4:4b). He is "the image of God"—i.e., the exact resemblance of the Father in His divine attributes, holy nature, and perfect love (Col. 1:15, Heb. 1:3). If we see Christ, we see the Father (John 14:7-10). *This* is what Paul preached—not himself, but Christ as the image of God (4:5). God who spoke physical light into existence (Gen. 1:3) is the same God who illuminated Paul and provided him with spiritual knowledge (4:6).[38] "[T]he glory of God in the face of Christ" means: the Father's own glory is seen by all who behold (in faith) His Son. "Miners carry a lamp on the forehead, Christians carry one in their hearts lit by the Spirit of God."[39]

The Difficulties Paul Faced (4:7–15): Even though he was a minister of a great "treasure" (the gospel) and deferred to the "greatness of [God's] power," Paul was just an "earthen vessel" (4:7; see 2 Tim. 2:20–21). As such, he continually faced difficulties and hardships which would have been insurmountable if not for the power that worked within him (Col. 1:25–29). He paints a grim picture on one side but a very inspiring one on the other (4:8–10):

Paul's burden:	God's provisional support:
"we are afflicted in every way"	"we are afflicted in every way"
"perplexed" [lit., to be at a loss (mentally)][40] over what is happening	"but not despairing" of all hope
"persecuted" by unbelievers and enemies within the church	"but not forsaken" by God
"struck [or, cast] down" by men	"but not destroyed" by them

The idea of "always carrying about in the body the dying of Jesus"[41] (4:10) may have more than one meaning. In one sense, Paul proclaimed the bodily death of Christ as part of his gospel (1 Cor. 2:2). Paul was not a pallbearer, but a preacher; he was not a eulogist, but an evangelist of the good news of salvation which came (paradoxically) through the horror of crucifixion as well as the victory of resurrection from the dead. In his *own body*—that is, through the physical, personal, and visible act of preaching the gospel—Paul "carried about" both the death *and* resurrection of Jesus Christ.

In another sense, Paul may be referring to the suffering he has borne *as the result of* preaching the gospel (4:10–11). In this view, the same *kind* of treatment that Jesus endured as a witness of God's truth, Paul endured as His apostle. Jesus suffered incomprehensible loss in coming to this world; Paul suffered "the loss of all things" in coming to the Lord (Phil. 3:7–9). Jesus bore stripes; Paul also bore the "brand-marks" of being beaten for Him (Gal. 6:17). Jesus was crucified *for* the world; Paul was crucified *to* the world (Gal. 6:14). Paul, in his own body, embraced "the fellowship of His sufferings, being conformed to His death" (Phil. 3:10). None of this puts Paul's suffering on par with Christ's, nor equates the exact experiences of suffering between the two men. However, it is true that Paul did follow in the footsteps of the Savior, and suffering for the gospel is the result of this decision. Yet, it is not all about suffering and loss: Jesus' virtuous life corresponds to the believer's "newness of life" in Christ (Rom. 6:4; see also Gal. 2:20).

Paul and others live in constant danger of death (1 Cor. 15:31) but serve as ministers to a Living Savior. Thus, "death works in us, but life in you" (4:12)—i.e., we are braving death so that you might hear the message of life. Jesus laid down His life to take it up again (John 10:17–18); the servant of Christ lays down his life for the brethren (1 John 3:16) in order that Christ will raise him up (4:13–14).[42] The same power that raised Christ from the dead will certainly raise to glory all those who believe in Him.

Such boldness of faith—in what God has done as well as what He has promised—Christians can communicate this message boldly to others. The Corinthians benefited from Paul's conviction of faith, having received the message he spoke to them. If *they* remain faithful as Paul is, *they too* will receive in the reward ("Jesus will present us with you"—4:14b). Thus, "All things are for your sakes" (4:15; see 1 Cor. 3:21–22). In fact, *many people*—including us—can enjoy the message of God's grace due to Paul's preaching and that of many other unnamed servants.

The Temporal and the Eternal (4:16–18): Given such hope and expectation, "we do not lose heart" (4:16), which brings the discussion back to where he began (recall 4:1). In this entire passage (4:16–18), we see a series of contrasts:

- ❏ decaying → renewal day by day
- ❏ outer man → inner man
- ❏ momentary → eternal (relative to duration)
- ❏ light → weight
- ❏ affliction → glory
- ❏ things seen → things not seen (or, visible → invisible)
- ❏ temporal → eternal (relative to time)

The "outer man" refers to one's physical body and the human condition in the earthly context. The "inner man" refers to one's soul (or heart) in the spiritual context. The physical body, and the world itself, is in the process of "decaying," indicating its temporary and transient nature. Things do not get increasingly better; instead, things are in a constant state of falling apart; this is true in the material world as it is with the physical human body. With increased age, we have decreased ability, mobility, and strength.

This inward renewal refers to a spiritual transformation, not a feeling or sensation. It involves the steadfast and active faith of the believer *coupled with* the divine energy that comes from God alone (see Rom. 12:1–2, Eph. 4:20–24, Col. 3:1–4, etc.). The effect of God's grace and truth upon his heart refreshes the believer's soul and renews his mind. While the physical life decreases and diminishes, the spiritual life increases in awareness, illumination, strength, and intensity. This "day by day" rejuvenation indicates a regular and perpetual process, not a once–in–a–while spurt of growth followed by a period of inactivity or disinterest.

The hardships of earthly life (and the demands of discipleship—Mat. 16:24), while seeming to overwhelm us now, are negligible in comparison to the glory and reward that awaits those who remain faithful to Christ until death (4:17–18). What we face now may seem neither "momentary" nor "light," but in comparison to the eternity to come it is infinitesimally small. The profound and immeasurable *weight of glory* far overwhelms the momentary *lightness of hardship*. This also implies: the believer should not avoid or ignore the hardships of discipleship to Christ if he desires the reward that follows. "The Christian who neglects duties and shirks responsibilities will find himself unqualified for the honors and glories God has in reserve for his faithful servants."[43]

Paul says, in essence, if you can see it, it will not last (4:18). This is true not only of the physical domain of humankind but of the entire universe.[44] Human faith does not rest upon what is seen but what is not seen (Heb. 11:1–3). Just as God made the present world out of nothing, so it will return to nothing; the visible and material realm is indeed passing away (1 John 2:15–17). Only human souls, while presently tethered to this world, will continue to exist in the world to come—the spiritual domain. There is a great paradox here: what we "look at" is invisible yet will become *more* visible than what we see in this world; and what we *think* is real (in this world) will soon give way to the *true* reality which is the spiritual realm (God's world).

Questions

1.) God's word repeatedly encourages believers not to "lose heart" (4:1; see John 14:1, 16:33, Gal. 6:9, Heb. 6:11–12, and 10:35–39). What exactly does it mean to "lose heart"? What does it look like?

   a. What does God promise to those who do *not* lose heart?

   b. What does God promise to those who *do* lose heart?

2.) Does Satan *obscure* the truth, or does he hinder the human heart from *receiving* the truth (4:3–4)? Is Satan able to overcome a person's free will to choose or reject God's truth? Please explain.

3.) Paul said, "For we do not preach ourselves" (4:5). How might a person preach himself today? Is this problem limited to actual preachers, or is any Christian capable of this?

4.) Paul said, "we also believe, therefore we also speak" (4:13). To what does this "speaking" refer? Are *all* Christians expected to "speak" what they believe? (Consider Mat. 10:32–33, Rom. 10:9–10, and 1 Pet. 2:9 in your answer.)

5.) How is one's "inner man ... being renewed day by day" (4:16)? Is this renewal produced by the believer, by God, or both? How do you know one way or the other? (Consider Rom. 12:1–2, Eph. 4:20–24, and Col. 3:9–10 in your answer.)

Lesson Five:
Our Future Glory through the Ministry of Reconciliation (5:1–21)

A Dwelling from Heaven (5:1–5): Anything that is human *made* or human *corrupted* will eventually be "torn down"—it will either die (Rom 8:13) or God will destroy it in divine judgment (2 Pet. 3:10). This is what we see in the Genesis flood, the destruction of Sodom and Gomorrah, the destruction of the Jewish temple (586 BC), and the destruction of the Jewish system (AD 70). But Paul's emphasis here (5:1–4) is not on the condemnation of specific sin, but the general *consequence* of sin upon humanity: the "earthly tent" (physical body) does not last forever; death has become a natural and unavoidable aspect of human life. The physical body is the "house" for our spirit, made to dwell in a three-dimensional material world.

But God's world does not accommodate a flesh–and–blood existence (1 Cor. 15:50). To live there requires that a believer to receive a new body "not made with hands." This new "building" (or "house" for the spirit) will accommodate a completely spiritual existence, one that is "eternal in the heavens" (5:1). Meanwhile, we "groan" in our physical body (5:2a) because the body requires constant care and attention; the aging process brings pain and magnifies our limitations; the "burden" of earthly life is difficult to bear (5:4). Not only do we *anticipate* something far better, but God has *promised* us something far better.

Just because we will not have a flesh-and-blood body in the spiritual realm does not mean that we will be *bodiless*—the essential meaning here of being "naked" and "unclothed" (5:2b–4). (Some ancient Greek philosophers believed that, upon death, a person's existence simply "atomized" into nothingness. No doubt some Corinthians were influenced by this teaching and may have even taught it within the church.) To be "clothed" not only takes away the shame and awkwardness of being "naked" but also implies *identity* with the one who clothes us (as in Rom. 13:14 and Gal. 3:27). In the afterlife, we will not simply be a floating, disembodied spirit that has no specific form or identity.[45] Instead, we will be given a new and glorified body that corresponds with the glory of the spiritual realm (1 Cor. 15:40–49).[46] At that time, "what is mortal will be swallowed up by life" (5:4)—that is, the physical, earth-bound human existence will, upon leaving this earth in death, be completely absorbed by and transformed into the essence of *heavenly* life.

Such comments (in 5:1–4) not only build upon what Paul has just said (in 4:18), but most certainly are an extension of what he has already said to the Corinthians concerning the bodily resurrection of the dead (1 Cor. 15:35–58). Regardless, Paul provides assurance that God is already preparing us to enter that heavenly existence (5:5). It is the Spirit's sanctification that makes this preparation—i.e., the transformation necessary to be so prepared requires nothing less than an act of God. Since we have God's Spirit given to us as a "pledge" (recall 1:21–22), we can be confident we are being prepared for a spiritual existence in the hereafter.

At Home with the Lord (5:6–10): "Therefore, being always of good courage" (5:6)—lit., of good cheer; having a sure confidence. Because of what awaits him, the Christian can serve the Lord, and even *suffer* for Him. Paul admits that while we are presently "at home" in the human body (because of where our "house" dwells), this means we are not yet in God's presence. Yet, because of the surety of God's faithfulness and His promises (1 Cor. 1:9, 2 Cor. 1:18), the believer can "walk by faith, and not by sight" (5:7)—i.e., we can have great confidence in what is coming because of the One who promises to provide it. "Sight" refers to a physical perception of earthly forms; faith refers to a spiritual conviction in heavenly realities. Whatever is seen (visible) is of this world; whatever is not seen (invisible) belongs to the spiritual realm (recall 4:18).

The things of this world will influence those who live according *to* the world; those who walk with God fix their attention on a realm that transcends this world. While the believer longs to be "at home with the Lord" rather than "at home" in the physical body (5:8), he must first demonstrate faith and courage while here in this life. Otherwise, he is not "prepared" for the life to come.

"Therefore"—since all that has been said so far is *true*—"our ambition" is "to be pleasing to Him" (5:9). This sums up the believer's life and purpose; any *other* life and any *lesser* purpose does not serve the Father's will, and thus is not pleasing to Him (Mat. 7:21). Regardless of whether we are here (in this human body) or there (in our glorified heavenly body), our *earnest striving* must be to find favor with God, which requires conformity to His Son (compare John 8:29 and Rom. 8:29). This is especially important since we will have our presentation *before* His Son in the Judgment (5:10; see John 5:22-24). At that time, we will answer for all that we have done, whether good or bad (Rom. 2:5-11, Rev. 22:12).

Paul's statement (5:10) is a general one that applies to *all* people, not only believers. We will not merely make an appearance before the tribunal of Christ; rather, He will expose us for who we really are on that occasion.[47] Christ will vindicate true believers; He will unmask hypocrites and false teachers; in either case, He will be the impartial Judge (as in Mat. 25:31-46). "Recompense" carries the idea of *receiving* what is due us, whether a reward or punishment, depending on our standing with God when we die.[48] Those who are "prepared … for this very purpose" (recall 5:5) have nothing to fear in this future event.

Controlled by the Love of Christ (5:11-15): Knowing that all men will one day stand before the Lord in judgment, "we persuade men" to hear and obey Him (5:11). This persuasion, in the form of preaching the gospel of Christ, is completely "manifest" (or, open to; seen by) God—Paul has no reason to hide or be ashamed of it—but he hopes that the Corinthians see it as well (recall 4:2). Instead of trying to justify his actions to the Corinthians, he wants them to be *proud* of what he is doing (5:12). The reasons for this: first, the salvation they have enjoyed through his preaching (1 Cor. 15:1-2), others who hear this message can enjoy this salvation as well. Second, the Corinthians can support Paul when his opponents criticize him (Mat. 26:10, in principle).

Regardless of what others have said negatively about him, Paul's conscience is clear, and the Lord has justified him (5:13; see 1 Cor. 4:1-5). Even if Paul and his fellow preachers are "beside ourselves" [lit., out of one's mind], the Corinthians still benefit from his work.[49] He is being facetious, of course, to contrast the even greater benefit of being of a "sound mind." Even so, he is making a serious point: it is not the *messenger* that matters as much as the *message* (Phil. 1:15–18). Paul is not insane, driven by human ambition, or under demonic influence; instead, nothing less than the "love of Christ" governs and compels his mind (5:14a).

People also accused Christ of being insane and demon-possessed (John 8:48, 10:20), yet the Father personally justified Him (Mat. 17:5) and the Spirit vindicated Him (1 Tim. 3:16). His love for men led Him to die for them (and us!), but through His death He brought life to "all" (5:14b). In other words, regardless of what people think of Him, Christ works to the benefit of all men (John 3:16).[50] He not only "taste[d] death for everyone" (Heb. 2:9), but His death serves as the "once for all" satisfaction for divine justice against our sins (Heb. 10:10–12).

"[T]herefore all died" (5:14b) means: not only did Christ die to save all those who obey Him, but these must also "die"—to sin, the flesh, the world, and even to themselves (Rom. 6:2, 11). Those who are "in Christ" are united with Him "in the likeness of His death" (Rom. 6:5) to enjoy *life* with Him (2 Tim. 2:11). Just as Paul no longer lived for himself (Gal. 2:20), so Christians are to live for Christ and not themselves (5:15). Christ died for us; we also are to "die" for Him. Likewise, as Christ "rose" from the dead to *live* for us, so He has resurrected us from our "death" (of spiritual condemnation) to "walk in newness of life" with Him (Rom. 6:4). The word of God speaks clearly and prolifically concerning this.

The Ministry of Reconciliation (5:16–21): Having newly introduced the subject of Christ's death and resurrection, Paul uses this opportunity to say even more about Him (5:16–20). Christ has ascended into the heavenly realm (Acts 1:9–11) and taken His seat at the right hand of God (Acts 2:33). He *was* once known in the "flesh" (John 1:14), but He is no longer a physical man, nor is He a dead man (5:16); "He has risen" (Mt 28:6) and God has glorified Him (Phil. 2:9–11). "We" once knew Christ in the flesh—as a man, a fellow human being—but all that has changed. Paul's point is that while he himself is still in the flesh (at the time of this letter's writing), his message concerns One whose existence *transcends* and is therefore *superior to* a flesh-and-blood existence. People can say what they want about Paul (he implies), but they have no good reason to say anything against the One whom he preaches.

Not only has Christ's relationship to the world changed (upon His death, burial, resurrection, and ascension to heaven), but so has one's relationship to the world changed once he is "in Christ." Paul has used the phrase "in Christ" extensively in his epistles, and it always refers to the same thing: a state of being in fellowship with God *through* the intercession of Jesus Christ. It necessarily implies a covenant relationship since this is the context in which the believer enjoys fellowship *and* intercession. And it speaks of a group of human souls—people who remain on earth as well as those who have already died—who comprise a spiritual body of believers we know simply as "the body" of Christ or "His church" (Col. 1:18).

One who is "in Christ" is no longer known (to the world) as he was before. He is changed; he is now a "new creature [or, creation]" (5:17). This describes one who is "created [anew] in Christ Jesus for good works" (Eph. 2:10). It is not the soul that is "new," for one does not receive a different soul upon his conversion; rather, it is the relationship with God that is new, being based upon terms and conditions that were not necessary before that soul sinned against God (see more comments below). The change or transformation that Christ underwent in His resurrection foreshadows the transformation one undergoes in his own spiritual resurrection to newness of life. The "old things" did not die for the believer (since they do still exist), but the believer has died to *them* (Rom. 7:4–6). His allegiance has changed; he no longer gives loyalty to the wicked impulses of the carnal mind, but now gives his heart to Christ who purchased him and to whom he now belongs (1 Cor. 6:20). "New things" are those which people cannot create; only God can create truly "new things," just as He spoke the world into existence out of nothing (Rom. 4:17, Heb. 11:3).

Instead of One who once "became flesh, and dwelt among us" (John 1:14), Christ now serves as a Living Redeemer in whom one finds reconciliation with God (5:18; see Rom 5:1–11). "Reconciliation" [lit., to be made friends with again] refers to the process by which God delivers one from his state of spiritual condemnation and brings him back into His fellowship—a fellowship that is far superior to what he once had in his childish innocence and simplicity. It is superior because now: he *knows* what it means to defy God; he has *experienced* the fallen condition of one who has defied Him, including the *terrifying judgment* that awaits all sinners; he has also tasted of the *heavenly gift* of salvation (Heb. 6:4–5); and he has *chosen* to be born again as a Christian, rather than simply being born of the flesh as a human being (John 1:12–13).

Reconciliation is the re–establishment of a relationship that has been severed—albeit on new terms, given what caused it to be severed in the first place. While reconciliation and forgiveness are similar in nature, and both seek the same objective, they are not interchangeable: forgiveness always focuses on whatever sin negatively affects the relationship, while reconciliation focuses on the relationship itself. God *forgives* us of our sins so that we can have fellowship with Him once again. He cannot reconcile to Himself anyone whom He has not forgiven; yet everyone whom God forgives, He also reconciles to Himself.

Reconciliation is a gift of God made possible through the atoning blood of Christ *and* the sanctification of the Holy Spirit (5:18; see 1 Cor. 6:11 and 1 Pet. 1:2). We are not reconciling God to us—we, having sinned, are not able to do this—but God is reconciling *us* to *Him*. We are the ones who have severed our relationship with God in the first place through our sin; therefore, it is we who need to be reconciled to Him, not Him to us. "The world" indicates not a fact, but an availability: in other words, the entire world is not reconciled to God just because Jesus died for it; however, everyone *in* the world does have opportunity to be reconciled *because* He died (1 John 2:2). Once we are reconciled, God no longer recognizes the sins which were once counted against us; the "word [lit., gospel; ministry] of reconciliation" has erased them forever.

Paul's point here: he is not the one who oversees the reconciling—that is God's business, as carried out through His Son—but he is an ambassador of this message (5:20). "Ambassador" comes from the same root word from which we get "elder" (5:20).[51] The meaning here is that of taking charge, to act as a representative, as an older man is often called upon to do.[52] While many preachers today might think themselves "ambassadors" in the same sense that Paul regards himself, this is not an equal comparison. It has nothing to do with age, *per se*, but with a level of responsibility. Christ entrusted His apostles with a responsibility that far exceeds that of any preacher today.

Paul's pleading with the Corinthians to "be reconciled to God" might seem an odd thing to say to Christians. Yet it is a general statement, not a specific one: he says what always needs done, not necessarily what has *yet* to do. He is not saying here, "Become Christians!" because they already are. But he *is* saying, in so many words, "Remain faithful to what it *means* to become Christians," for such admonition is ever relevant and is the subject of many pulpit sermons today.

Christ is the essential factor in the process of reconciliation to God (5:21). He did not *become sinful* to provide this reconciliation, but He did take upon Himself the *penalty* of sin—which was death (1 Pet. 2:22, 3:18). Since Christ was numbered *among* the transgressors (Isa. 53:12, Luke 22:37, Gal. 3:13), people might believe that He *was* one. Yet, if He had sinned against God, then it would be impossible for Him to offer Himself as a worthy sin offering on our behalf. Instead, He identified with sinners without succumbing to the *weakness* of men and the temptation to sin. This does *not* mean that He takes responsibility for our sins, for this remains forever ours. Rather, He has provided the *sacrifice* necessary to atone for our sins so that we might regain our innocence before God (Col. 1:19–22). Because of what He has done for us, therefore we can "become the righteousness of God in Him."

Questions

1.) Why do Christians struggle with the idea of a spiritual body in the hereafter (5:1)? (There are several answers.) How can we respond to or resolve this struggle?

2.) Paul says that God is the One who has "prepared us for [the] very purpose" of receiving an immortal body in the hereafter (5:5). What exactly needs to be "prepared"? Do we have any responsibility in this preparation? Please explain.

3.) For many centuries, churches and church officials have used the Judgment Day to terrify and intimidate people into submission (to such men, if nothing else). Is this what Paul is doing (in 5:10)? If so, how does this fit the context (5:1–10)? If not, why does he bring it up at all?

4.) "Therefore if anyone is in Christ, he is a new creature; the old things passed away; behold, new things have come" (5:17). What "old things" have passed away? What "new things have come"?

Lesson Six:
The Genuineness of Paul's Ministry
(6:1—7:1)

The Difficulties of Being God's Servants (6:1–10): In this next chapter, Paul continues to expound upon his role as an "ambassador" for Christ (recall 5:20). This is done not only to give the Corinthians a better glimpse into this role, but to respond to those in that congregation that commend themselves by their status (likely, as teachers of Judaism) or abilities (as master rhetoricians). To devalue or reject an apostle of Christ is to reject the message of reconciliation that Christ provides. To "receive the grace of God in vain" (6:1) is to commit to this message but then rob it of its purpose and its transforming power.

Self-commendation—the practice of those in Corinth who are bad-mouthing Paul—defeats the benefits of grace, for they are no longer honoring God but commending themselves.[53] The Corinthians are in the same danger that Paul revealed to the Galatians: they once accepted God's help, but now they are rebuffing God's ambassador—and thus, they are trusting in themselves rather than God. Paul (6:2, quoting Isa. 49:8) reminds them that God alone can save men: He is the only One who can help us; salvation is impossible otherwise (Mat. 19:26, John 15:5).[54] There is a sense of urgency to all this, however: the "acceptable time" indicates one should not neglect or procrastinate toward this window of opportunity (compare Isa. 55:6–7 and 2 Pet. 3:9). Paul is urging the Corinthians to *listen to him* as an ambassador of Christ, and not to regard him as expendable—or worse, *an enemy* (Gal. 4:16). He expected the Corinthians to surrender to the grace of God immediately, without delay or exception. Paul and his fellow workers "[give] no cause for offense in anything" (6:3)—i.e., they are conducting themselves properly, and therefore ought not to be accused of any wrongdoing.

Paul took his ministry very seriously and has already repeatedly proven his willingness to suffer for the cause of Christ. He "commends" himself as a servant of God (6:4)—not by his own estimation, credentials, or conscience, but because of the stewardship entrusted to him. (He has already explained this in 1 Cor. 4:1–16 but is about to revisit that thought in the present passage.) To illustrate his commitment to Christ and the ministry of reconciliation which Christ made possible, Paul produces a list of physical hardships that he has endured and continues to endure on behalf of the recipients of this ministry (6:4b–5):

- **General hardships:** "afflictions," "hardships," and "distresses." These are things that Paul has faced "with much endurance," meaning they were extremely difficult ordeals. The book of *Acts* (13—28) details such scenarios that Paul had to endure.
- **Troubles with the law:** "beatings," "imprisonments," and "tumults" (i.e., situations of civil disorder). These troubles were not because Paul was engaging in criminal activity, but because others accused him of being a lawbreaker (as in Acts 16:16–24), or because people used the law to carry out their vendetta against him (as in Acts 21:27–36).
- **Physical struggles:** "labors," "sleeplessness," and "hunger." While undergoing various "hardships" and troubles with the law mentioned above, Paul has suffered personally and physically in these ordeals.

All said, preaching of the ministry of reconciliation (the gospel) has taken a personal toll upon Paul (and others). Despite this, he does not allow self-pity or victimhood to interfere with the great responsibility entrusted to him to present the gospel message appropriately. Thus, he now describes the honorable *way* he preached Christ's gospel (6:6–7):

- "in purity"—untainted by pride or the pursuit of personal gain (recall 2:17).
- "in knowledge"—not his, but that which was revealed to him (Gal. 1:11–12).
- "in patience [or, longsuffering]"—i.e., he recognized (and was patient toward) the difficulty people had with hearing the gospel for the first time, and/or internalizing its message (2 Tim. 2:24–26, 4:2).
- "in kindness"—not out of spite, nor with self-vindication or arrogance (unlike those who have been discrediting him).
- "in the Holy Spirit"—i.e., by His authority; according to His will; in compliance with His direction. This means *divine action* is involved with the preaching of Christ's gospel—in the form of visible miraculous

confirmation (2 Cor. 12:12) or in other ways that God chooses to "mightily [work] within" Paul (Col. 1:29).
- "in genuine [or, unfeigned; sincere] love" [Greek, *agape*]—acting in the best interests of others, even at a loss to himself (1 Cor. 13:4-7, 1 Pet. 1:22).
- "in the word of truth"—i.e., according to the genuine gospel that has been revealed by God, by which one is redeemed (Eph. 1:13–14) and "born again" (1 Pet. 1:23).
- "in the power of God"—because the proclamation of Christ's gospel is useless and irrelevant unless confirmed by demonstrations of otherworldly power and authority (i.e., miracles; see Rom. 15:18–19, 1 Cor. 2:4, 2 Cor. 12:12, 1 Thess. 1:5, etc.).
- "by the weapons of righteousness…"—an allusion to a well-armed Roman soldier who is prepared for both defensive and offensive battle. While Paul's "weapons" here are spiritual in nature, they are nonetheless real and effective (Rom. 6:13, Eph. 6:10–18).

Such is the way Paul has presented the gospel of Christ. His ministry has been honorable, decent, and full of integrity. Nonetheless, not everyone "sees" him in this positive light; some view him negatively, as one who does not know what he is talking about, as weak and ineloquent (see 10:10), or as someone to be despised. So then, Paul now describes the different *receptions* people have had about him as a preacher and an apostle (6:8–10):

- "by glory and dishonor"—his preaching was well-received by some, but disdained and discredited by others (see Acts 13:44–52 for this contrast).
- "by evil report and good report"—some slandered Paul, while others spoke well of him.
- "{regarded} as deceivers and yet true"—some characterized Paul as a master deceiver (which he addresses later), and yet his gospel could not be refuted, nor could his apostleship be diminished. Jesus' own words were "full of grace and truth" (John 1:14), yet certain Jews also accused of being a "deceiver" (Mat. 27:63).
- "as unknown yet well-known"—Paul was unknown by many (a "nobody"—2 Cor. 12:11); because he was not known to the leading Judaizers, he lacked credentials and status among them. However, his

preaching was turning the Roman world upside–down (Acts 17:6 and 28:21–22).
- ❑ "as dying yet ... we live"—Paul narrowly escaped death many times (recall 4:11); by all accounts, he should never have survived as long as he did. And yet—"behold!"—he is most certainly alive.
- ❑ "as punished [lit., chastened; disciplined] yet not put to death"—not punished by God, but by men who thought they were doing God a favor (John 16:2–3), or who were angry over Paul's interference (as in Acts 16:19–21).
- ❑ "as sorrowful yet always rejoicing"—Paul and his companions have many reasons to bemoan their circumstances and hardships; the Corinthians themselves have been the source of much grief. Yet, Paul regards his situation with joy and draws tremendous comfort from the mercies of God (recall 1:3–4).
- ❑ "as poor yet making many rich"—while Paul has nothing to offer in the way of earthly wealth, the spiritual treasures which he shares with many are priceless and incorruptible. In the same way, Jesus appeared poor on earth (2 Cor. 8:9) but distributes great spiritual wealth to all who come to Him (Heb. 11:37–38).
- ❑ "as having nothing yet possessing all things"—having lost his identity with the world (Mat. 16:25, Gal. 2:20), Paul has become an heir of "all things" through Jesus Christ.

Such are the paradoxical contrasts of how a false teacher (or unbeliever) viewed Paul and how Christ viewed him. To some, Paul has no right to preach the gospel; he is a pathetic man whose "personal presence is unimpressive, and his speech contemptible" (2 Cor. 10:10). But in Christ's eyes, Paul has been doing exactly what He wanted him to do—and will be well–rewarded for this in time.

Paul's Plea for the Corinthians' Reception (6:11–13): Paul has been straightforward and unpretentious toward the Corinthians. However, those whom he has tried so hard to help have not reciprocated his kindness (6:11–13). As his "mouth" is open, so is his heart. He has withheld nothing from the Corinthians, but they have withheld their full expression of love and fellowship from him. While this certainly has caused Paul grief, the Corinthians are really hurting themselves the most. He regards them as "children" either in reference to their immaturity, or because he is their "father through the gospel" (1 Cor. 4:15), or both. In his fatherly role, Paul has the right to expect a respectful and appreciative response.

Communion with God vs. Friendship with the World (6:14—7:1): Having come out of worldly backgrounds, the Corinthians remain heavily influenced by worldly teachings and expectations. Such worldliness (including the attitudes that accompany it) has no connection with Christian fellowship and behavior. Paul, in essence, is linking the two problems: their struggle with worldliness itself and their refusal to open wide their heart to him because they listen to worldly-minded men (i.e., those who challenged his authority and sought their own agendas). Paul has shared with these people a gospel of light; they are still associating with darkness by listening to those who are leading them astray. Paul says, in the clearest language possible, that there can be no coexistence between these two spiritual worlds.

We note the various facets of relationship stated here (6:14–16): "bound together"; "partnership"; "fellowship"; "harmony"; "in common"; and "agreement." In every example given, Paul provides two ideas that are incompatible.[55] He is not saying such spiritual unions are unlikely, bad, or inadvisable; he says they *cannot happen*. While it is true that people can and do enter unholy earthly unions (e.g., a contract, relationship, marriage, etc.), God gives no approval for a Christian to create a *spiritual* union with anyone who stands opposed to Him. To attempt to do this anyway puts the Christian in league with Satan, not Christ. While Paul puts this teaching in the form of rhetorical questions, we can rephrase them as direct statements:

- Believers are not to be "bound together" with unbelievers.[56]
- Righteousness has no partnership with lawlessness (1 Thess. 5:21–22).
- Light has no fellowship with darkness (1 John 1:5).
- Christ has no harmony with Belial [lit., "a worthless person"; a synonym for Satan].
- Believers have nothing in common (spiritually speaking) with unbelievers.
- The temple of God has no agreement with the temple of idols (1 Cor. 8:5–6, 10:21).

The context for *all* these incompatible things is spiritual, not literal. Paul is not saying, for example, "Christians are not to have anything to do with unbelievers, lawless people, those who walk in moral darkness, etc." These are the very people whom we are seeking to *save*, not avoid; in fact, we (Christians) were once one of them (Eph. 2:1–3, Titus 3:3). Instead, Paul says: do not enter into any agreement, alliance, or fellowship with those who will compromise your primary allegiance with the Lord. Entering any union with an unbeliever—or worse, a false teacher—is an attempt to join *Christ* to that person in an unholy way and through a perverse relationship.[57] If anyone wishes to "come after" Christ, he must renounce the world and its darkness, not join himself to it (John 3:18–21, Mat. 16:24–25).

Again, while the context in which Paul speaks is spiritual in nature, this does not mean that the *manifestation* of such unions always remains spiritual. For example, if a Christian takes a job that demands he attend cocktail parties with clients or provide illegal favors for them to get their business, the invisible spiritual union has manifested itself in a visible manner. "Time and time again in the early Church, the choice came to people between the security of their jobs and their loyalty to Jesus Christ."[58] The Christian's association with Christ forbids being in league with Satan under any circumstances. One's relationship with God precludes all others (i.e., that would hinder this one). Thus, the separation of which Paul speaks may also bear upon one's family life, one's circle of friends, or one's social life. Christ said that He must be followed above *all others*, no matter how close to us they may be (Mat. 10:34–37, Luke 9:59–60, and 14:25–26). While such a separation can be extremely painful, it is one to which every believer has already agreed in his decision to follow Christ.

"For we are the temple of the living God" (6:16a)—"we" likely refers to the brotherhood of Christ (all Christians), but it can also be understood individually (1 Cor. 6:19–20) and congregationally (1 Cor. 3:16). In any case, God will not partner with evil; Christ and Satan cannot walk together; wherever the Holy Spirit "dwells," evil cannot be present. One who is "born of God" (John 1:12–13) cannot be in league with any person or teaching that will compromise his relationship with the Father.

"Temple" References:	
The **individual** believer is a "temple"	"Or do you not know that your body is a temple of the Holy Spirit who is in you … ?" (1 Cor. 6:19)
A **congregation** of God's people is a "temple"	"Do you not know that you are a temple of God and that the Spirit of God dwells in you?" (1 Cor. 3:16)
The entire **brotherhood** of Christians is a "temple"	"For we are the temple of the living God …" (2 Cor. 6:16; see Eph. 2:19–22, 1 Pet. 2:4–5)

This phrase, "I will be their God, and they shall be My people" (6:16b), may well be the thesis statement of the entire Bible. It shows the objective for why God created human beings in the first place, and what the purpose of every human being is supposed to be. This speaks of God's desire for *fellowship* with men—not only in this life, or for a brief time, but throughout the eternity to come. "God is faithful" to His people (1 Cor. 1:9) but the Corinthians—and covenant believers everywhere—must also be faithful (6:17–18). "[C]ome out of their midst and be separate" means:

- no longer be identified with those who oppose Christ and His teaching.
- no longer be influenced by such people; do not make binding covenants (literal or figurative) with such people that will violate your allegiance to Christ.
- expose the darkness of the world for what it is—the realm of Satan—rather than enter fellowship with it (Eph. 5:7–12).[59]

The *object* of faithfulness—God's and ours—is the covenant into which we have entered with the Lord, which Christ's blood brought to life (Mat. 26:28, Heb. 9:13–26). God will be faithful to His covenant, but we must be faithful to it as well. God guarantees His promises to us, but He requires that we remain faithful to *our* promises to Him:

We are the temple of the Living God God will dwell in us He will walk among us He will be our God We shall be His people He will welcome us He will be a Father to us We shall be "sons" to Him	**IF**	we are not bound with unbelievers. we are not partnered with evil. we do not walk in darkness. we do not fellowship with Satan. we do not live like unbelievers. we do not practice idolatry (of any kind). we separate ourselves from worldliness. we do not "touch" what is unclean.

Paul finishes this parenthetical thought (begun in 6:14) in 7:1: "Therefore, having these promises"—i.e., God's promises of dwelling among us and making us His people (or possession; Titus 2:14)—we are supposed to live like those who have *received* such promises and who have made our *own* promises to the Lord. In obedience, then, we are to "cleanse ourselves from all defilement of flesh and spirit"—i.e., purge our lives of anything that stands in the way of a pure relationship with God, as well as any darkness that may still linger in our hearts. "Perfecting holiness" is reminiscent of priestly service in which priests render homage, offer sacrifices, and represent God to the world (Rom. 12:1–2, 1 Pet. 1:13–16, and 2:4–9). "Fear of God" does not mean being *afraid* of Him but showing reverence and offering worship (Acts 10:35).

Questions

1.) What does the fact that one *can* "receive the grace of God in vain" (6:1) necessarily imply? Is grace a guaranteed gift of God or a conditional one? Please explain.

2.) Please compare 6:7 with Eph. 6:17 and Heb. 4:12. What is the purpose of "the word of truth"? Is it a defensive or an offensive weapon—i.e., is it meant to protect or destroy? Is it possible that it can be used in both ways at the same time?

3.) Paul provides contrasting views of how others perceive him (6:8–10). Is it possible that someone might characterize your actions as *good* while another sees the same action as *bad*? Consider this in view of the following scenarios:

   a. You miss a Sunday night assembly to attend your daughter's high school graduation ceremony.

   b. You invite a friend (who is not a Christian) to services, and as the communion trays pass by him, he partakes of the emblems—and you do nothing to prevent this at the time.

   c. You buy your daughter a beautiful pastel dress to wear for the first time to services on Easter Sunday.

   d. An adult who was baptized when she was 10 years old is convinced in her heart that she needs to be baptized again, and after a discussion on what the Scriptures teach concerning baptism, you perform this for her (or at least give your visible support to this).

e. A 10-year-old child comes to you and tells you he wants to be baptized, but you counsel him to wait until he is more mature to make such an important decision.

4.) How does each Christian need to apply the "come out from their midst and be separate…and do not touch what is unclean" instruction (6:17) in:

   a. movies he (or she) watches?
   b. books or magazines he reads?
   c. music (and lyrics) he listens to?
   d. internet sites he visits?
   e. social or recreational activities he engages in?
   f. friends he keeps?
   g. language (i.e., choice of words) he uses?
   h. behavior he displays to others?

5.) Why is it important to view God as our "Father" and ourselves as His "sons and daughters" (6:18)? What positive effect should this have on our *fellowship* with Him?

Lesson Seven: Paul's Appeal for the Corinthians' Affection (7:2–16)

Paul Pours Out His Heart to the Corinthians (7:1–7): Having taken a moment to address *why* the Corinthians had restrained their love toward him, Paul now implores again that they would reconsider this. "Make room for us {in your hearts}…" (7:2)—i.e., there is no good reason why the Corinthians could not or should not trust his sincerity and selfless motives. He has done nothing to warrant their having withheld their love from him. He reaffirms his own true and honorable disposition toward them. He is willing to lay down his life for them, if necessary, but what he really seeks is for them to *live* as fellow believers (7:3).[60] Even though they have often acted like children (1 Cor. 3:1–3), Paul is proud of how much they *had* matured and has great "confidence" in them (7:4). Even so, there remains a conspicuous reluctance to receive Paul fully and without reservation. He is asking, in essence: Why won't you put confidence in me, since I have suffered so much for your sake?

To underscore his care and concern for the Corinthians, Paul recalls again the anxiety he experienced when he arrived in Macedonia without having heard from Titus (7:5–16; recall 2:12–13). Paul had written a long and difficult letter to the church (what we call "1 Corinthians"), and he was anxious over news of their reception concerning it.

Titus, one of Paul's protégés, was the key communication link between Corinth and the apostle at this time. Titus had been working directly with the Corinthians in trying to help them resolve their struggle against Paul, and it is likely that he had borne the alleged "sorrowful" letter to them as well. Thus, Paul experienced "conflicts without, fears within" (7:5)—i.e., the external hardships of travel and his ministry as well as the internal turmoil within his heart over how the Corinthians would receive his letter. As a manifestation of God's comfort to the apostle, Titus finally reunited with Paul (7:6–7, 13; recall 1:3–7). Titus himself found great comfort in the favorable report of the Corinthians' reception of Paul's letter.

Paul's Angst over Writing His Letter (7:8–12): Paul now describes the conflicting emotions he experienced during that time (7:8–12); the disjointed and sometimes awkward writing in this section indicates Paul's highly emotional state of mind. He did not regret—but he once *did* regret—sending the letter, since it provoked the Corinthians to do what was necessary to rectify the problems he had addressed.

While his letter had caused them sorrow, this was necessary to induce the proper response: their repentance. This *kind* of sorrow serves the will of God (7:9) and contributes to the salvation of the one doing the repenting. The "sorrow of the world" is unconcerned with repentance; instead, it dwells upon feelings of guilt, shame, and emotional distress for having been exposed as a wrongdoer (7:10). This distress might be due to the loss of status, another's trust, friendships, or material possessions; these are all things of the world, not of God. Such superficial "sorrow" does not lead to salvation but "produces death"—i.e., it does not change one's status of condemnation before God (Rom. 6:23) but only compounds the problem. "Sorrow for sin is to see sin as God sees it."[61]

The sorrow that Paul caused the Corinthians, however, was only temporary, and led to the correction of their problems—i.e., true reform, not emotional distress. "Repentance" involves both a change of *attitude* as well as a change in *action*. It is the reformation of one's heart that leads to a restoration of one's fellowship with God, and thus with His people. Paul expresses changes of the Corinthians' *actions* based upon their change of *attitude* (7:11):

- "godly sorrow"—instead of being arrogant as before (cf. 1 Cor. 5:2), the Corinthians have manifested genuine mourning toward their sins and have taken appropriate action.
- "vindication of yourselves"—this speaks to their eagerness to clear themselves of any wrongdoing. The Greek word here is *apologia*, from which we get "apology," used here in the formal sense (as a defense of one's position).[62]
- "indignation"—they showed righteous anger toward the sins among them, those who had incited the apostle's rebuke, and those who had led them into believing what was false.

- ❏ "fear"—likely, this refers to the Corinthians' respect for God's authority.
- ❏ "longing"—the object of this longing is unclear, but it likely refers to their desire to see Paul (implied in 7:7), have his censure of them removed, be further instructed by him, or all of these.
- ❏ "zeal"—their earnestness in wanting to do what is right, regardless of the cost or consequences, which is the basic meaning of "moral excellence" (2 Pet. 1:5).
- ❏ "avenging of wrong"—not *personal* vengeance, but carrying out *God's* vengeance in the form of whatever discipline is required among their members.

"In everything you demonstrated yourselves to be innocent in the matter" (7:11b): the Corinthians *proved* their change of heart through actions that were consistent with such change. Put another way: the good fruit that they bore vindicated their sincerity. The identity of the "offended" and "offender" (in 7:12) remains unknown to us for certain, but it is sufficient that Paul and the Corinthians both know. Paul admits that the positive change in the *congregation* is more important than the details of incidental situations that had existed among them.

Titus' Favorable Report (7:13–16): As it is, Titus has brought an overall favorable report of the Corinthians' response to Paul's letter. Because of this, not only is Paul relieved and refreshed, but so is Titus himself. This also means that Paul's boasting about the Corinthians (to Titus and others) has not been in vain; they have responded just as he had hoped (and predicted) they would. The Corinthians' obedience (7:15) was worth all the time and energy Paul and Titus had expended toward them.[63] Now Paul can "rejoice" over his confidence in them rather than having to further rebuke and discipline them.

Questions

1.) To "make room" in their hearts for Paul (7:1), what did the Corinthians need to do *first*? Is this action also necessary to "make room" for Christ? Please explain.

2.) Paul was glad for the Corinthian's sorrow, "in order that you might not suffer loss in anything through us" (7:9). What "loss" is he referring to in this context? Do *we* suffer loss when we fail to repent of our sins? Please explain.

3.) How does the "sorrow of the world [produce] death" (7:10)? Why does the sorrow according to the will of God produce life? If we demonstrate no godly sorrow for sin, will God forgive us anyway?

4.) The Corinthians' obedience brought Titus welcomed joy (7:15), even though their obedience was to God and not to himself. Should we also be joyful over another's obedience to God? (Consider Rom. 16:19, Phil. 2:1–2, 2 John 1:4, and 3 John 1:3–4 in your answer.)

Section Two:
Monetary Collection and
Principles of Giving
(8:1—9:15)

Lesson Eight:
Paul Reminds the Corinthians
of Their Pledge (8:1–24)

The Macedonians' Fine Example (8:1–5): Having commended them for what they *had* done, Paul now must address that which the Corinthians have *yet* to do. They had promised a year earlier to contribute to the needs of the saints in Jerusalem who were suffering from famine in that region (see Rom. 15:22–28). In his previous letter, Paul had instructed the members to set aside this money every first day of the week (1 Cor. 16:1–2). However, it is clear (no doubt based on news from Titus) that they have not followed through with this commitment, forcing Paul to have to address the matter. The way he does so, however, is tactful, discreet, and allows the church to shine in obedience rather than face a withering rebuke from him. He approaches the Corinthians in a positive way yet without ducking the necessary admonition.

Paul begins by commending not the Corinthians but their brethren to the north: the Macedonians (8:1–5). (This included, at least, the brethren in Philippi, Thessalonica, and Berea—churches that Paul had established on his so-called second missionary journey; see Acts 16:9—17:15.) These brethren have endured much affliction from the Jews (1 Thess. 1:6–9, 2 Thess. 1:4), as well as "deep poverty."[64] Even so, they have given liberally and cheerfully to the relief effort of the church in Jerusalem, which has suffered years of famine, social unrest, and political instability. In fact, the Macedonian Christians begged Paul to let them help "in the support of the saints," even to their own hurt, and even beyond what Paul expected.

"The grace of God" is what inspired such giving: as God had given much to the Macedonians, they were determined to give freely to others (8:1).[65] In doing so, they put God's work ahead of their own interests ("they *first* gave themselves to the Lord"—emphasis added), which is a powerful testament to their devotion to God and His people. Such an attitude will necessarily manifest itself in visible charity and a desire to contribute to the sacred work of the church.

The Corinthians' Need for Follow-through (8:6–15): The Corinthians, meanwhile, have become distracted with other things. They had the means to help, but they did not necessarily have the same priorities as seen in the Macedonians. Titus had helped them in the past to organize their contributions, and now Paul will send him back to Corinth to "complete in you this gracious work" (8:6). Paul compliments first ("you abound in everything," etc.), then provides instruction: give to *this* need as abundantly as you do in these other areas (8:7). The instruction to finish this commitment is based upon their own promise to help; it is not a mandate or command from Paul (8:8).[66] As they have been earnest in other matters, they need to be earnest in keeping their promises, too.

While Jesus was rich with heavenly glory, He became poor with earthly humility for our sakes (8:9). As the Corinthians have profited from His generous and selfless giving, so others will benefit from theirs. In Paul's opinion, "this is to your advantage" (8:10)—i.e., you will profit spiritually from that which you give materially. While it might seem better to cling to earthly wealth as a means of security, protection, and resourcefulness, the opposite is true regarding the spiritual work of the church. Paul reminds them not only of their year-old commitment to help but also the godly desire that inspired that commitment.

Charitable contributions shared among God's people will take care of those who are in need, due to the generous providence of God Himself (8:12–15). God never asks us to give what we do *not* have but to share what we *do* have (8:12). And such giving is *never* meant to afflict one group to take away from the responsibility of another group (8:13). Rather, it is to allow *both* groups—the one with something to give as well as the one that is in need—to trust God will provide for them.

All this is a basic biblical principle that began with Israel's system of tithing and other contributions (as in Num. 18:21–32, Deut. 14:27–29, and 24:19–21), and which continues today in Christ's church. And, as Jewish Christians in Paul's day contributed to the spiritual welfare of the Gentiles, so Gentile Christians can contribute to the material needs of their Jewish brethren. In this way, a balance will be struck: no church will have too much, and no church will have too little (8:14).[67] Likewise, no church will have to give too much (without being re-supplied by God), and no church will have to receive too little (since God's provisions are inexhaustible). The OT quote (in 8:15) is from Exod. 16:18 in reference to Israel's gathering of manna: no one was to gather more than he needed, but neither was anyone to gather *less* than this. As God was the supplier of manna, so He is now the supplier of all the wealth—material, financial, and otherwise—of His people.

The "Brothers" Who Will Accompany the Gift (8:16–24): Paul does not need to persuade Titus to bring this work to a close, for he himself is already eager to see it done (8:16–17). With such self-initiation, Titus is ready to leave for Corinth to oversee the completion of this work; in fact, it appears (from 8:6) that Titus is the bearer of what we are calling the "2 Corinthians" letter. "We are often surprised how slow Christians are to do work without a living voice to encourage them, but it seems to have been the same in Paul's day. He could not trust his letters [alone] to stir them up to activity."[68] Not only will Titus be leaving soon for Corinth, but another unnamed brother will accompany him (8:18–19). The identity of Titus' traveling companion, the "brother whose fame in ... the gospel," is unknown to us for certain, and may be someone altogether unfamiliar to us. This man has been "appointed by the churches" because of his good character and reputation.

The reason for him accompanying Titus is so that no one will accuse Paul or Titus—or a collaboration of the two of them—of extortion, or of fleecing the congregation for their own purposes (8:20–21; see 1 Cor. 16:3–4).[69] (Paul has already been accused of such things and will address these accusations later in this letter.) Again, Paul did not choose this unnamed brother but "the churches" chose him. Yet another unnamed brother—again, someone whose identity we do not know—will also escort Titus (8:22), but Paul chose this man himself. This second unnamed brother has been "tested" (or, proven; approved; examined) by Paul and his fellow workers over time and found to be genuine and reliable. It is possible that this is Luke, a regular traveling companion of Paul's.[70] Since Paul's reputation is on the line here, it is important that he send very capable and trustworthy men to carry out a work to which he has given his—and, more importantly, the Lord's—blessing.

Titus is the same one to whom Paul wrote "Titus" in our NT. Here, as in that epistle, Paul gives a high commendation of this man. Here (8:23) Paul calls him "my partner and fellow-worker"; in Titus 1:4, he refers to him also as "my true child in a common faith." Likewise, the other two brothers in Christ who will escort Titus "are messengers [lit., apostles] of the churches," whose integrity is solid and genuine. (Apostle, in this context, is used in a general sense, not with reference to the *office* of an apostle, to which Paul was called; recall 1:1.) These men are not only conducting important work for Paul, but they are also "a glory to Christ" because they are serving the needs of His people. For this reason, he expects the Corinthians—with all the other churches watching—to receive such men well, and to show them the Christian love they deserve (8:24).

Questions

1.) The Macedonian Christians begged Paul to let them participate in the support of the saints (8:4). Why would they do this, especially since they themselves were impoverished? Can—and should—the same thing(s) that motivated them also motivate us to support fellow believers?

2.) Paul says the Macedonians "first gave themselves to the Lord and to us by the will of God" (8:5; see Phil. 4:14–17). Why is this attitude necessary *before* one contributes any dollar amount to the Lord's work? What if it is missing?

3.) What is the relationship between *giving* (as a contribution) and *fellowship*—with God *and* His saints?

   a. Is spiritual fellowship possible apart from any personal and measurable contribution?

   b. For Jesus to have fellowship with us, did He make a personal and measurable contribution *to* that fellowship (8:9)?

4.) Paul took great pains to ensure that no one could make any provable accusations against him regarding the money he collected (8:20–21). Should we continue this practice in our own handling of the saints' collections? Can this principle also apply to how we conduct ourselves in the sight of others (consider Titus 2:6–8, for example)?

Lesson Nine:
Principles of Charitable Contributions
(9:1–15)

Paul Urges the Corinthians to Act (9:1–5): Chapter nine continues to address the subject begun in 8:1. Paul admits that it is needless ("superfluous") to have to detail the "ministry" (of the contributions to those in need) for the Corinthians—they already know of it (9:1). Their initial zeal concerning this contribution a year earlier had prompted other churches to participate in it as well (9:2).[71] However, since then, the Macedonian churches have far exceeded the Corinthians in responding to it (recall 8:1–5). Meanwhile, the Corinthians have been dragging their feet (for whatever reason), and Paul is saying, in so many words, that they have procrastinated long enough.[72] He had spoken well to the Macedonians of the generosity of Achaia (of which Corinth was the capital), yet this would be an empty boast if Corinth did not follow through with their commitment (9:3–4).

Paul employs some motivational psychology here—positive peer pressure—to instill in the Corinthians a sense of urgency to act (9:5). He says some "Macedonians [might] come with me," and if the Corinthians are not prepared with their contribution by that time, it will be an embarrassment for all of them. Paul boasted about the Corinthians' liberality before having seen it, but he has already stated his "confidence" (recall 7:16) that they will perform as expected. The "brethren" who are going on ahead of Paul's visit refers to Titus and the two other unnamed workers (recall 8:16–22). "Bountiful gift [or, bounty; blessing]" refers to a proper commendation, blessing (in reference to people), or praise (in reference to God).[73] Their gift would be a *blessing* to those in need of it, and a form of *praise* to God. Paul does warn them, however, against allowing "covetousness" [lit., greed] to compromise their generosity.

A "Cheerful Giver" (9:6–9): Leaving behind the reference to the specific contribution to the Christians in Judea itself, Paul now speaks to the general principles of giving. He begins proverbially with a principle that extends far beyond mere monetary contributions (9:6; see Prov. 11:24, Eccles. 11:1–6,

Luke 6:38, and Gal. 6:7). *How* one gives (whether bountifully or sparingly) is the direct result of *why* one gives (motive); the hand is conditioned by the heart. If one's motive is to seek gain through the Lord, then he will give generously; if his motive is to seek gain in this world, then he will give sparingly.[74] One will never "reap" the intended *benefits* of sacrifice if he refuses to *make* one.

But Paul's point here (9:6) concerns not only the amount one *gives*; it also concerns what he will *receive*. Giving to the church is like planting and sowing seed. If a farmer sows few seeds, he will harvest a small crop; if he sows much seed, this naturally increases the expectation of the crop. As in the natural world, so it is in the spiritual realm: if we are tight-fisted and miserly with our giving to God and others, then God will withhold His blessings from us; if we are generous and benevolent in our giving, then He will respond in like manner.[75] "Giving" here must not be limited to monetary contributions, although it most certainly includes them (since this *is* the subject at hand). All forms of giving are determined by the heart of the one who gives them, regardless of the nature of the specific gift. For example, if we are tight-fisted (so to speak) with how we evaluate the motives or actions of others, then God will use our overly critical approach against *us*; if we are generous and merciful toward others, He will be merciful to us. As we judge, so He will judge us (Mat. 7:1–2, Jas. 2:13).

Voluntary, freewill offerings are always superior (in quality) to those required by law (9:7). Likewise, a cheerfully given gift is always superior to those given sourly, regretfully, or begrudgingly. "[P]urposed in his heart" indicates the true source of one's giving: it is not about the quantity of his gift, but the quality of it, as a reflection of his heart.[76] In other words, Paul draws the Corinthians' attention to the condition of their hearts, not to the actual dollar amount of their contributions. One who gives liberally indicates confidence in God to balance the "equality" (recall 8:13), though not necessarily in monetary compensation. One who gives sparingly indicates a failure to trust in God's system of sacrifice and blessing. Each person puts his trust in his own control and prosperity, or he trusts in God's heavenly providence; each person makes his own choice in the matter of giving.

"God loves a cheerful giver" (9:7)—and who doesn't? "Cheerful" here means happy, joyful, and (by implication) grateful (cf. Rom. 12:8).[77] The focus here is on the nature (or heart) of the *giver*, not the gift itself. One should not be made cheerful only because he put a check in the plate, so to speak; it should be a cheerfully benevolent heart that inspires all such donations. And how does God respond to the cheerful giver? In essence, *however He chooses to*, but always to the great benefit of that person. God is "able"—powerful, capable, infinitely resourceful—to bring about all sorts of abundance to those who trust in His system of sacrifice and compensation (9:8; see Eph. 3:20–21 and Phil. 4:18–19). "Grace" here does not refer to saving grace, but it does refer to what is given to those who are *being* saved. In this case, "grace" refers to God's kindness, favor, gifts, or blessings in whatever form He provides them. Just as His *saving* grace is all-sufficient for salvation (2 Cor. 12:9), so His *provisional* grace is all-sufficient for whatever need is present in the life of the cheerful giver.

All said, we never need *more* than what He will provide, but He needs us to trust that He *will* provide, as He has promised. Just as God desires cheerful giving, so He provides "an abundance for every good deed." What God *can* do, He *will* do for the one who trusts in Him (9:9, quoted from Psalm 112:9). The psalmist describes the character of the righteous man; Paul says that this is also the character of a righteous God. And, in the context of the subject at hand, a righteous man will trust that a righteous God will take care of *him* as he "scatters abroad" to *others*.

God Is the Source of All Increase (9:10–15): Natural laws of agriculture provide excellent analogies for spiritual lessons (9:10–11), which is why Jesus used them frequently in His own parables. The farming analogies here (seed, sowing, reaping, and harvest) may not seem immediately relevant to those not living in an agrarian society, but they certainly are to the Corinthians whose sustenance depends upon a good crop. Just as the farmer sows seed in hope of a good harvest, so the Christian sows "seed" in the fields of ministry to God. Just as God provides seed for one crop which produces seed for a future planting, so He provides sufficiently for those whose wealth is diminished through generous giving (Isa. 55:10). God, the supplier for and completion of *all* spiritual needs, gives abundantly so that those who receive may be "enriched in everything for all liberality"—i.e., He is generous to *them* so that they may be generous to *others*.

Financial benevolence is not the only form of gifts, offerings, and contributions. God is glorified also through the "many thanksgivings" offered up to Him by recipients of such kindness (9:12). "The ministry of this service" seems redundant at first, but refers to the process of (or, the service of) benevolence in all of its forms.[78] God is glorified through the "obedience" and "confession" of those who make sacrifices in His name, while those in need are blessed through their generosity (9:13). The *proof* of this obedience and confession is in the gift itself.

Paul is not just raising money for a good cause here. He is using this contribution as a means of *uniting* the two groups—Gentile and Jewish Christians. Thus, predominantly Gentile churches are helping Jewish Christians in ways that not even wealthy Jews would do for their own kind! And while the Corinthians give their gifts to their fellow brethren in need, God continues to give the gift of His saving grace to the Corinthians (9:14). No wonder, then, Paul ends this section with praise for *God's* gift over and above the Corinthians' gifts (9:15; recall 2:14).

Questions

1.) Was it appropriate for Paul to use peer pressure to motivate the Corinthians to finish what they started (9:1–5)? If so, can we do this today with our own brethren? If not, what is wrong with this?

2.) How might the Corinthian's "bountiful gift" (i.e., their contribution) be "affected by covetousness" (9:5)? How might *our* contributions be affected in this same way?

3.) In 1 Cor. 16:2, Paul describes the quantity of one's contribution ("as he may prosper"); in 2 Cor. 9:7, he describes the quality of it ("as he has purposed in his heart"). Is one of these more important than the other, or are they equally important? Please explain.

4.) Why does God bless one person so they may share with another person who is in need? Why do you suppose He does not simply bless the one in need directly, and bypass the middleman (so to speak) altogether?

5.) In 9:1 and 9:12, the recipients of the contribution are clearly stated. Who are they?

   a. Is this always the case with collections of money in the NT church?

   b. Should the church be collecting money for the needs of those other than that for which we have clear precedent?

SECTION THREE: PAUL'S DEFENSE OF HIS APOSTLESHIP (10:1—13:10)

Lesson Ten: Paul's Response to His Accusers (10:1–18)

The Warfare of the "Flesh" (10:1–6): A distinct and (some have said) surprising break in tone and content occurs in *2 Corinthians* between chapters 1—9 and 10—13. Most likely, Paul is simply shifting gears, so to speak, to address a different group of people within the Corinthian church than he had been addressing so far. (This view will be the position of this workbook.)

While Paul has had many good things to say about the Corinthian church overall, there remains within it a group of men who regarded him *personally* with contempt. These men have not only questioned his apostolic authority; they have attacked his character and integrity. Such attacks, left unaddressed, undermine his leadership and credibility, and therefore he cannot ignore them. The exact *expression* of these attacks is not clear, except from what we learn through the text of this section (chapters 10—13). Paul feels compelled not only to vindicate himself but also the apostolic office in general, which requires exposing the errors of a false apostle.[79] (The evidence he presents will still refute those who claim to be modern-day "apostles.")

Paul's opening comments (10:1–2) indicate great restraint, even though there is obviously a measure of sarcasm in his words. (Sarcasm, in this context, defines an appropriate literary device, and is not to be confused with its modern usage, which is often purposely belittling. In its purest literary sense, sarcasm is meant to expose the illogical conclusions of an opponent's argument to show the untenableness or absurdity of that person's position.) While he has been accused of being "meek" (or, lowly; subservient) and helpless to those who challenge him, Paul reminds these men that they are measuring him against the "flesh" (i.e., by worldly or human standards) rather than considering the spiritual power he possesses as an apostle (1 Cor. 4:20). His reference to Christ underscores his point: while in the flesh, Christ was humble, meek, and gentle (Mat. 11:29), yet His power and authority were greater than that of all His opponents—including Satan.

While Paul is obviously a man *of* flesh, he does not "war" (or, contend) according *to* the flesh—unlike the character of his accusers (10:3-4). "The flesh" (here) refers to the human condition in an earthly context. The "weapons of our warfare" involve both offensive and defensive powers entrusted to the apostles by the Holy Spirit, which he would use only when needed. Paul is not going to contend with his accusers on their level, according to their human resources or strategies, but—if necessary—will subdue them with power against which they cannot defend themselves. Such "weapons," being "divinely powerful," exceed the power or nature of this world and can defeat man–made "fortresses" (i.e., arguments based on human reasoning).

The knowledge of God (doctrine) *and* the power of Christ (authority) will destroy whatever raises itself up against Christ and His kingdom (10:5). "Speculations" here refers to wicked imaginations, false philosophies, or any intellectual resistance of the gospel.[80] "Lofty thing" refers to an opinion that poses as doctrine or something worthy of discussion. "Taking every thought captive to…Christ" is based on Christ's supremacy over all human wisdom. The idea of taking something "captive" indicates a *victory* over an opponent's assault and a *vanquishing* of that person's human power. Paul is not merely out to win arguments, however; his intention is to win souls, to bring people to obedience to Christ. He also wants his opponents in Corinth to humble themselves with repentance before carrying out any discipline against them (10:6).

An Inferior Standard of Measure (10:6–12): Those who challenged Paul compare themselves to him as men often compare themselves to other men. They sized up his physical strength; they looked upon his physical appearance; they critiqued his oratory skills. In all these areas, they thought themselves superior to him; thus, they assumed their spiritual knowledge and strength were also superior. Paul warns against such foolish reasoning, and he reprimands the rest of the group for having given these men the attention they crave. "You are looking at things as they are outwardly"—i.e., your standard of measurement is faulty and unreliable to begin with (10:7). These men who discredit Paul claim to belong to Christ yet are comfortable with condemning one of Christ's own apostles—a contradictory position. One does not support or give true allegiance to a leader by destroying those who speak in that leader's name. The Lord gave Paul authority with the intent to edify, not punish—although he can do both (10:8). His claim is not an empty one; his letters are not empty threats, although he does not write them merely to "terrify" anyone (10:9).

Yet, some have concluded that the only thing Paul can do *is* write letters, since his personal appearance and speech are deemed "unimpressive [or, weak]" and "contemptible" (10:10). "Unimpressive" here implies a sickly, diseased, or infirmed condition.[81] This is not necessarily based upon facts but is likely a purposely malicious mis-characterization designed to cast doubt and skepticism upon his credibility. They are attacking the *person* rather than the *argument*—a far easier strategy, as they see it.

Paul warns against drawing conclusions based upon human opinions— especially one's own. When the time comes, he will conduct himself just as powerfully in person as he does in writing (10:11). We should remember that he did not *want* to be absent but is giving the Corinthians time to repent before he visits them again (recall 1:15–24). We should also remember what Paul did to Elymas on the island of Cyprus when that man continued to stand in the way of Paul and Barnabas' preaching (see Acts 13:8–11).

Paul's opponents—whom he will later call "false apostles"—assumed they could contend with him on their own level. They assumed that, because they commended themselves, certainly he was doing the same thing—but not as successfully as they had done (10:12). Paul rebukes such comparisons as being characteristic of those "without understanding," since they wrongly assumed his true intentions, they being "swelled with an inflated sense of self–importance."[82] With a touch of sarcasm, Paul says, in essence, "Apparently I am not bold enough to do what these other men have done."

A Superior Standard of Measurement (10:13–18): Instead of measuring himself *by* himself, Paul defers to the measurement of any person "which

God appointed us as a measure" (10:13; see 1 Cor. 4:1–4). In other words, Paul did not have two different measurements—one that favored him, and another that was critical of his opponents—but one singular, impartial, and divinely-given standard by which to measure *all* men.

Paul then reminds those challenging him that *they* did not bring the gospel message to *him,* but he brought it to *them* (10:14; see Acts 18:1–11). In doing so, he did not overstep the boundaries or authority of his apostolic and evangelistic duties. The false teachers only took advantage of the work that others had done; they had no original work of their own. Instead, they were trying to claim authority over (and boast about) what Paul had started, not what they had done. Paul, on the other hand, did not build upon other men's work, but preached the gospel and established churches in places that had not yet been evangelized (Rom. 15:17–20). Yet, as the work in Corinth grows, it will enlarge the efforts first made by Paul to areas in which had yet to hear the gospel preached (10:15–16).

Paul has not been boasting *to* the Corinthians but (if anything) has been boasting *about* them. He refuses to boast in someone else's work, but he also does not want the Corinthians taking credit for *his* work. Ultimately, all boasting must be "in the Lord" (10:17; see 1 Cor. 1:31). No one has any right to take credit for what God alone can do, and He has done exceedingly beyond whatever mere men (including Paul) have accomplished.

God determines our standing with Him, not us. A person (Christian or otherwise) is not "commended [or, established; approved]" by his self-estimation but by God's estimation of Him (10:18). To be "commended" by God is to stand before Him justified, righteous, and in His fellowship, all due to Christ's redemption of that person's soul. The one whom God does *not* commend will not find any help in the day of judgment by resting upon his own boasting, self-glorying, or resting on his own accomplishments.

Questions

1.) How are "meekness" and "gentleness" (10:1) defined in a Christian context? How were those who resisted Paul interpreting these expressions differently? Does the world continue these same misrepresentations today?

2.) What are some "speculations" and "lofty things" *today* that need to be "destroyed," since they defy the revealed "knowledge of God" (10:5)? How exactly *are* we to "destroy" these things—or is this even our responsibility? Please explain.

3.) How were some Corinthians "looking at things as they are outwardly" (10:7)? Do Christians still do this today—look at things "outwardly" rather than with a spiritual (and transcendent) perspective? How might we do this in the following cases:

   a. Dealing with enemies and antagonists of Christians?

   b. Dealing with indifference and apathy among Christians?

   c. Confronting challenging situations, difficult personalities, and obstacles?

   d. Grappling with pain, human suffering, and the seeming unfairness of life?

   e. Facing one's own failing health, including one's own mortality?

4.) People might reach wrong—and even damaging—conclusions about you, just as some Corinthians did about Paul (10:10). Are you to respond in the exact same way Paul did—with warnings of punishments and destruction? Or is Paul's case entirely different than your own? Please explain.

Lesson Eleven:
Paul's Challenge to His Accusers
(11:1–33)

A Pure Betrothal (11:1–3): The "little foolishness" refers to the irony and kind of reasoning in which Paul engages to defend his apostleship and silence his detractors. It is "foolishness" because it compares Paul to these so-called apostles merely on the level of human achievement, as men are prone to measure things (11:1). He asks that, if he must go down this path, the congregation will hear him out, despite his uncomfortable position. But even in this, the apostle far exceeds the boastful claims of his accusers since their own efforts pale in comparison to what he has already accomplished—and endured—for Christ.

While Paul's accusers want the Corinthians to focus on them, Paul wants the Corinthians to focus on Christ (11:2). He came to these people not for his own personal advancement, but out of love for their souls. With "godly jealousy"—a strong desire for God to be the object of all human worship—he refused to let them be "betrothed" to any teacher or figure other than Christ, the Bridegroom of the church (Eph. 5:23–27). Paul rightfully assumed the role of a (spiritual) father to these people since he is the one who brought the gospel to them (1 Cor. 4:15). And, just as a father would oversee the betrothal of his daughter to her future husband, so Paul oversaw their spiritual union with Christ.[83] Yet, as Eve was seduced by the serpent's temptations,[84] the Corinthians have been seduced by the wicked temptations of those who challenged Paul and his authority (11:3; see Gen. 3:1–6 and 1 Tim. 2:14).

The Christian religion, Paul says, should be *simple* and *pure*, not complicated and/or corrupted with human teachings or expectations. Paul's accusers are trying to distort this simplicity and purity with worldly estimations, deceptions, craftiness, and ulterior motives. Such things lead people *astray* from the truth rather than keeping them *close* to it. These men are drawing the Corinthians to themselves rather than to Christ. At the same time, they are making it sound like this is what *Paul* is doing—drawing believers to himself, not Christ—and thus forces him to respond to such charges.

Paul Defends His Actions (11:4–12): Paul begins his defense by reprimanding the entire congregation's gullibility. Just as the Galatian Christians had allowed themselves to be "bewitched" by those who introduced to them "another gospel" (Gal. 1:6, 3:1), the Corinthians have also embraced teachings of those who are not commissioned by Christ and who preach a different gospel than what Paul revealed to them (11:4). "[Y]ou bear this beautifully [or, put up with it well enough[85]]" is not a compliment but a sad observation. The Corinthians did not defend either Paul or his gospel but patiently allowed certain men to lead them astray. Ironically, the Corinthians chose men with a different gospel and no credentials over the one who brought them the gospel in the first place and confirmed it with miracles and proofs of his apostleship (see 2 Cor. 12:12). These false apostles vaunt their status and oratory skills but have no *power* (1 Cor. 4:20). Paul calls these men's claims "foolishness," and if the Corinthians would bear with the foolishness of false preachers, then they ought to bear with *his* foolishness for a moment.

Paul refers to his accusers—those who have challenged his authority—as "eminent apostles [lit., super-apostles]" (11:5). These men were not content to be mere apostles on the same level as Paul but claimed to have *superior* status—one even greater than his own! Even so, Paul is not impressed and does not regard himself "inferior" to them. Even if they possessed superior oratory skills,[86] they did not possess superior "knowledge [of the Holy Spirit's revelations—MY WORDS]" (11:6). This lacking on the part of these "eminent apostles" should have been evident to the Corinthians; the difference was obvious if they had but paid attention.

Furthermore, Paul brought the gospel to them free of charge (11:7), whereas others were "peddling the word of God" for money (recall 2:17). His intent was not for personal gain but to bring the gospel to the Corinthians without letting money interfere with the process. Yet, the false apostles insinuated this to mean that since he *charged* nothing, Paul's preaching must be *worth* nothing.

The false teachers misinterpreted the situation. Paul *did* receive compensation, but not by the Corinthians. In fact, Paul "robbed other churches"[87] in order not to burden the Corinthians with his expenses (11:8–

9) and declined his legitimate right to payment for his services (see 1 Cor. 9:11–18). When necessary, he also worked with his own hands to provide for himself (Acts 18:1–3; see 2 Thess. 3:7–9). Paul's "boast" (11:10) was that he was able to provide the gospel free of charge to the Corinthians without placing any further burden upon them. The *news* of this provision went well beyond the borders of Achaia (Greece).

The reason for this provision was not because his gospel was not worth paying for but because of his great love *for* the gospel, for Christ, and for the Corinthians themselves (11:11). This love is authentic—so much so, that he calls God as his witness to its genuineness. And, he has no desire to change his method simply to gratify the desires of his accusers. Instead, he chooses to unmask the accusers for who they really are so that the Corinthians will no longer put any confidence in them and their words. They do *not* preach out of love but opportunity—for glory, control, and compensation (11:12). By exposing them as frauds, Paul will "cut off [their] opportunity" to put themselves in the same category as himself. At the same time, Paul himself is deeply hurt by those who hold his great generosity (in not charging the Corinthians for his preaching) in contempt.

Paul Unmasks His Accusers (11:13–20): Paul's letter at this point gets gritty; he minces no words and dispenses with all subtleties. "For such men are false apostles, deceitful workers, disguising themselves as apostles of Christ" (11:13)—this is bold and straightforward language, and is among the strongest in all of Paul's letters. It is like what Jesus said of the Jews and of Satan (in John 8:37–55). Indeed, these "eminent apostles" have aligned themselves with Satan, not Christ; their motives are satanic in nature, and do not serve God's interests (Mat. 16:23).

The early church was plagued with false apostles, false teachers, and false Jews (Acts 20:30, Phil. 3:2–3, 2 Pet. 2:1–3, Rev. 2:2, 9, etc.)—impostors all. These men infiltrated unsuspecting congregations and slowly poisoned them with smooth words and deceitful doctrines (Rom. 16:17–18, etc.). The "deceitful" nature of their work indicates ill–intent: they are not innocently mistaken in what they say but purposely mislead people to gain their trust, their following, and their money. "The servants of Satan do not hesitate to hold ecclesiastical offices, or occupy pulpits."[88]

Just as Satan can masquerade as "an angel of light," so his servants can pretend to be "servants of righteousness" (11:14–15). This is a frightening thing to consider. It demands that Christians everywhere remain vigilant of such danger and ready to expose it when confronted with it (Titus 1:9, in principle). Satan does not manifest himself to us openly but through crafty disguise—say, in the form of a pious helper, a charitable worker, or a so-called apostle—to infiltrate and manipulate a group of people to serve his own agenda. Their "deeds" will reveal them for what they really are (see Mat. 7:15–20).

Paul loathes the idea of stooping to the level of his accusers to defend himself, yet this seems the only way to get through to the Corinthians. His words (in 11:16) can be paraphrased as: "Don't think me a fool—but even if you do, receive me anyway. You've put up with the foolishness of others; why not put up with mine for a moment?" This is not how he typically speaks as an apostle, but the circumstances call for it (11:17). These false teachers boasted as though they had done great things for the Lord; Paul's "boasting" reveals a genuine and enduring devotion to the cause of Christ. Paul is about to show just how much he *believes* in his gospel by how much he has *suffered* for it.

The Corinthians have boasted about how "wise" they are (see 1 Cor. 4:7–8), yet they listen to foolish men and false teachers (11:19). These men enslave, devour, take advantage of, belittle, and even abuse the Corinthians (11:20)—things Paul *never did* and would *never do*.[89] In due time, these other men will fleece the congregation of its virtue, power, and resources to gratify their own self-serving appetites. Paul seems to speak in amazement that the Corinthians choose to give *so much* attention to those who have *so little* to offer.

The Remarkable Suffering Paul Has Endured (11:21–33): Paul admits (sarcastically) that he must appear "weak" to the Corinthians by not having boasted at all until now (11:21a). The false apostles have portrayed themselves as bold, devout, and caring men who have a better understanding of the gospel than he does. Yet, Paul is ready to unmask them by showing what a *genuine* apostle endures to hold that office (11:21b). While what follows is extremely difficult for him to engage in, Paul sees it necessary to establish—hopefully, for the last time—the level of service he has provided Christ and His people to preach His gospel.

This list of sufferings of Paul (11:22–29) is impressive, and nearly unimaginable. Perhaps no Christian at any time has so consistently and thoroughly endured so much for the Lord. What is also impressive is that this list deals only with what Paul has endured through Acts 20, the point in time in which he penned this epistle. Therefore, it does not include his trial and arrest in Jerusalem, the attempts on his life while in custody in Jerusalem, his imprisonment in Caesarea, his shipwreck on the journey to Rome (Acts 27), his imprisonment in Rome for two years, and all that occurred thereafter. Because of these things, he is not intimidated by those who oppose him; indeed, he can match and *exceed* their every boast with genuine acts of virtuous service.

Paul begins, however, with what the two—himself and the "super-apostles"—have in common (11:22). This is not for the purpose of finding common ground with these men, but to show that their boasts are, even on the most basic level, not superior to his own. In doing so, he also reveals the identity of these accusers: they are "Hebrews" and "Israelites"—i.e., they are *Jews* who are leveraging their ancient Jewish heritage against the pagan and spiritually-ignorant pasts of many of the Corinthians. These men wear their Jewish heritage as a badge of honor and superiority over the Gentile Corinthians; they smugly assume a position of authority founded upon a lineage that is traced back to Abraham (Gal. 3:7). While he has not pressed his Jewish privilege (see 1 Cor. 9:19–22), Paul nonetheless meets these false teachers point for point regarding nationality, heritage, and ancestry. But this is where the comparison ends.

In 11:23, Paul uses the superlative phrase "I far more so" as a means of leaving his accusers far behind regarding credentials. While these men *claimed* to be "servants of Christ," Paul, through the impressive listing of his trials and sufferings, the threats against his life, and the daily pressure that he endures, has *proven* to be a servant. It is not as though suffering by itself proves anything (since a person can suffer horribly for a useless cause), but that it so perfectly complements all his other "proofs" of apostleship—spiritual knowledge, miraculous ability, revelations from God, etc. This included:

- "labors" (11:23): perilous and difficult hardships associated with his apostleship, which include not only extensive and exhausting teaching, but also many refutations and confrontations.
- "imprisonments" (11:23): up until Acts 20, there is only one written account of Paul being imprisoned (in Philippi—Acts 16:22–40), but there were obviously others. Clement of Rome (late 1st century AD) claims that Paul was put in bondage seven times.[90]
- "beaten times without number [or, exceedingly in stripes]" (11:23): this refers to beatings of all kinds, some of which will be mentioned specifically in the next phrases.
- "in danger of death": this refers to any exposure to death, or being in any life-threatening situation.
- "thirty-nine lashings" (11:24): "lashings" (a.k.a. floggings; see Acts 5:40) refers to being whipped with a leather whip (or thong), a common punishment of the Jews. Paul claims that "five times" he endured this, but there is no such record of this in *Acts*, indicating (again) that Luke's account is not comprehensive regarding Paul's ministry, nor was it intended to be.
- "rods" (11:25): a common punishment of the Romans (Acts 16:22), akin to the modern "caning," in which a prisoner is whipped with flexible canes or thick vines (or something similar) rather than leather thongs. Either lashings or beatings with rods could cause death, either by inducing shock by loss of blood or from the extent of the injuries themselves.
- "stoned" (11:25): a form of ritual execution by the Jews in the case of blasphemy, according to the Law of Moses (Lev. 24:16). In this case, a crowd of men would push a victim into a pit outside the city and pummel him with stones (as they did to Paul in Lystra—Acts 14:19–20).
- "three times ... shipwrecked" (11:25): the only account of Paul being involved in a shipwreck is in Acts 27, which occurred after this writing. Nonetheless, due to "defective navigation and unskilled shipbuilding, and from want of the mariner's compass,"[91] shipwrecks were a constant risk among the ancient seafarers.
- "in the deep" (11:25): this may refer to being left adrift at sea alone, possibly while waiting to reach shore after a shipwreck. It also may refer to Paul clinging to a floating plank or fixture of a sunken ship, or its lost cargo, while waiting to be rescued.

Paul's account also illustrates the difficult times in which he lived (11:26–27). Life was hard in the ancient world; travel was even harder. Likely, this is foreign to us today. We feel like we are "suffering" when our flight is delayed, or our car has a flat tire. Traveling in the ancient world—and Paul literally traveled thousands of miles during his missionary journeys—endured the risk of armed bandits (think of Luke 10:30), natural obstacles (swollen rivers, storms, etc.), wild animals, the loss of one's provisions and luggage, disease (such as malaria), and deadly exposure to the elements. It was expensive, physically exhausting, and extremely time-consuming; death was not uncommon.

Paul also faced the added threat of religious opponents—some of whom sought his life (as in Acts 14:4–7 and 23:12–15)—and other opponents as well (as in Acts 16:19–24). Everywhere he went—every province, every city, and every congregation—Paul had to watch his back. There were many "dangers" awaiting him everywhere he went: in the city, on the road, at sea, and even among "false brethren" who were like wolves in sheep's clothing. "[L]abor and hardship" indicates the personal toll that traveling and dealing with difficult people and situations have taken on him. Along with this, Paul has endured "many sleepless nights" out of concern for the brethren and his own safety. Food and water were difficult to obtain on the road in the ancient world, and he often found himself wanting for both. Likewise, keeping warm with scant clothing was a constant struggle. Likely, Paul had a bundle of personal belongings he had to carry with him wherever he went, which was often insufficient for his personal comfort.

As if all this were not enough, Paul endured daunting concern for the churches—a responsibility that weighed upon him even during times of relative peace (11:28). His "intense concern" for the weak never let up; new converts to the faith were vulnerable to many temptations, and he prayed for them earnestly and went from "house to house" to ground them in the faith (Acts 20:20). Paul endured external threats as well as internal distress; he was a man virtually consumed by his ministry. It was only by the grace of God that he was able to endure—and survive—as long as he did (1 Cor. 15:10).

Paul's "boasting" is not to pat himself on the back for all that he has done but to show how *human* he is, and how *difficult* it has been to conduct the Lord's work (11:30). The false teachers in Corinth liked to fancy themselves as "apostles," but they have not been *called* as apostles, and most certainly have not *served*—or even *suffered*—as apostles. Not only this, but he calls upon "The God and Father of our Lord Jesus" as a witness to the facts and sincerity of what he has just detailed (11:31).[92]

As a possible example of a particular instance of weakness, Paul recounts his deliverance from Damascus by being let down through a hole in the wall (11:32–33, alluding to the account in Acts 9:23–25).[93] While it is obvious Paul's life was in danger, he regards that experience as a time when he let his personal and very human fear get the best of him.[94] Perhaps he saw this as a moment of failing to trust in God for deliverance. While this hardly seems "weak" to us (under the circumstances), an intensely driven, passionately devout man as Paul will regard it as such.

Questions

1.) Paul explained that the Corinthians were being deceived and led astray in their "minds" (just as Eve had been) without even mentioning their actions (11:3). What does this tell us about where any departure from the "simplicity and purity" of the gospel begins?

2.) Paul laid a heavy condemnation against those who disregarded his apostolic authority, calling them "false apostles, deceitful workers," and masqueraders of righteous men (11:13–15).

   a. Does this same condemnation apply today to church leaders (in *any* church) who claim to be "Christians" but refuse to submit to apostolic authority? Why or why not?

   b. Is anyone with whom you disagree over Scripture considered a false teacher and a "deceitful worker"? If so, why? If not, why not?

3.) Consider what the NT says about Satan:

   - "we are not ignorant of his schemes." (2 Cor. 2:11)
   - "our gospel ... is veiled to those who are perishing, in whose case the god of this world has blinded the minds of the unbelieving." (2 Cor. 4:3–4)
   - "even Satan disguises himself as an angel of light." (2 Cor. 11:14)
   - "And you were dead in your trespasses and sins, in which you formerly walked according to the ... prince of the power of the air." (Eph. 2:1–2)
   - "Your adversary, the devil, prowls about like a roaring lion, seeking someone to devour." (1 Pet. 5:8)
   - "The whole world lies in the power of the evil one." (1 John 5:19)

Considering these things, how should you regard Satan? What "power" does he have?

4.) Paul's list of sufferings (11:23–29) is both impressive and humbling. Yet, are we supposed to feel unworthy of our own ministry to Christ because we have not suffered as much as he did? On the other hand, what value is our ministry *without* suffering (see Rom. 8:16–17, Jas. 1:12, 1 Pet. 3:13–15, 4:12–13, etc.)?

Lesson Twelve:
Visions and a "Thorn"
(12:1–13)

Visions of Paradise (12:1–6): Having been lowered down from a wall in Damascus, he now turns to "a man" who has been raised up to the highest heights (12:1–6).[95] Undoubtedly speaking of himself (see 12:7), Paul speaks in the third person due to the nature of the "boasting"—i.e., it is nothing for which he can personally take credit. Paul did have a choice in all the previously mentioned experiences; this vision, however, was something done *for* him, not by him.[96] He provides the account of a historical experience, but not an explanation of it. His point might be paraphrased in the first person: "Before you (Corinthians) were entertaining the so-called 'super apostles'—before you were even a church!—I was already receiving heavenly visions from the Lord." He was not trying to exalt himself, since it took him fourteen years to even disclose it, but to shame the Corinthians. Furthermore, the false apostles might be claiming to have visions from God, but their character lacked credibility and sincerity, thus casting tremendous doubt on all such claims

Paul describes a "vision" that he received "fourteen years ago"—one that completely overwhelmed him ("in the body or apart from the body, I do not know") (12:2a). Given the date of this letter (ca. AD 57), this would have been ca. AD 43, several years after his conversion.[97] We have no idea where Paul was when this happened, except that it occurred while he had gone into Arabia and Damascus—a time in his post-conversion life that remains largely unaccounted for (Gal. 1:17). We also do not know for what specific reason he received this vision, except to say that Christ deemed it necessary to embolden him to face the many trials and ordeals He knew lay ahead of him (see Acts 9:15–16). Paul himself is uncertain as to whether he participated in the vision *bodily* (like the "trance" he recalls in Acts 22:17) or *spiritually*—that is, in some non-physical manner, as if his *consciously aware* of one place while his body remained in another. (For example, compare Rev. 1:9 and 4:1–2, where John faced a similar experience.)

Paul says he was "caught up [lit., snatched; seized with eagerness]" into the "third heaven" (12:2b). The ancient Jews spoke of three "heavens": the first was the earthly atmosphere; the second, the domain of the stars, sun, and planets; the third, the spiritual realm where God dwells. The "third heaven" is the general context; "Paradise" is the more specific description. The word "paradise" means "garden," "park," or "cultivated area." In the spiritual context, "Paradise" (a proper name) refers to the dwelling place of the blessed (Luke 23:43, Rev. 2:7).[98] Being carried into this "third heaven"/"Paradise," Paul heard "inexpressible [or, unspeakable] words." These are not words Paul could not understand but that he had no permission to repeat (as in Rev. 10:4). God revealed these words for Paul's edification and/or consolation, and only he *himself* could hear and know them.

Paul mentions such "visions and revelations" (recall 12:1) only because he knows that none of the so-called "most eminent apostles" (recall 11:5) have ever had them. He will boast "on behalf" of the man whom God took to Paradise—a veiled reference to himself—only because he was not responsible for making this happen (12:5). "For if I do wish to boast…" (12:6)—i.e., Paul has every right to boast about this, since what he says is true. Yet, he chooses not to do so that he may not receive credit for what he is unable to perform. This is why he defers to the "I know a man" designation rather than speak about himself directly.

God's Power Is Perfected in Paul's Weakness (12:7–10): This next section (12:7–10) is one of the most potent and revealing passages in this entire letter—or even the entire NT. God brought Paul up (in a vision) to see Paradise and hear "inexpressible" words spoken there. This is an extremely rare privilege that few men on earth have ever received. Yet, "to keep me from exalting myself" (12:7), Paul also received a "thorn in the flesh"— something to keep him humble, to remind him of his human condition, and to prevent him from boasting about his visions. While it might seem cruel that God allowed his most prized servant to be afflicted in this way, Paul saw the matter quite differently.

Speculations abound as to the identity of this "thorn in the flesh."[99] It might have been a physical malady, impairment, or impediment of some kind; a common belief is that Paul had some sort of eye trouble, based upon Acts 9:9 and Gal. 4:14–15. Or, it may have been the persistent and unrelenting assault of the Judaists, always trying to tweak and misrepresent what Paul preached. Obviously, it is something that we will never know (for certain), are not meant to know, and do not need to know. The phrase "a messenger of Satan to torment me" has also received numerous interpretations, none of which seem completely explanatory or satisfying.[100] Perhaps it is enough to realize that while God *permitted* the "thorn," Satan is the one who *inflicted* it. Also, this "tormenting" situation, whatever it was, had a debilitating effect on Paul.

Paul did make a sufficient request ("three times") to have this "thorn" removed (12:8). This does not necessarily indicate three separate prayers but implies three separate rounds or series of prayers—a full, complete petition (parallel to Jesus' threefold petition in Mat. 26:36–46). God did not, however, remove the "thorn" but spoke instead of His grace and power, and how He manifested these through Paul's ordeal (12:9).[101] "Grace" is not merely God's kindness (or, beneficence), which He shows to all people (Mat. 5:45), but the special providential care given only to those who belong to Him in Christ.[102]

God's answer reveals that Paul's suffering would lead to greater gain (for Paul, and particularly for the Lord *through* him) than he would have enjoyed by having it removed. Paul asks from what he *thinks* is best; God responds from what He *knows* is best. The sufficiency of His grace implies the sovereignty of His decision: He speaks from a position of the highest authority, not as an equal who assesses Paul's situation no better than he can do himself. And, God does not apologize for His answer, for He has done no wrong and has made no mistake in providing it.

"[P]ower is perfected in weakness"[103] is an obvious paradox yet so succinctly and beautifully describes God's divine power in relation to the frail human condition. It is not until we recognize our own weaknesses that we will learn to trust in God's unfailing power. God supplies power to address the need, not to exalt—or even spare—the one who is in need. While false apostles boast in their own power, even claiming to invoke the "power of God" in their preaching (think of the modern-day "faith healer"), God declares that

He magnifies His power through human weakness (1 Cor. 1:18–25). Though he would rather have had the "thorn" removed, Paul understood the message: "when I am weak, then I am strong" (12:10). He was thus willing to suffer his "thorn in the flesh"—and whatever else he needs to endure—if indeed Christ is honored through his faithful obedience to Him. To "boast about" his weaknesses is to magnify all that Christ accomplishes through him *despite* such weaknesses. The word "dwell" here means to "tent upon," "abide with," or "rest upon."[104] Christ's abiding presence is all-sufficient for Paul; he needs no other blessing.

Paul Lays Bare His Intentions (12:11–13): The Corinthians' quick desertion of Paul's teaching "compelled" him to become "foolish" to reassert himself as a legitimate apostle appointed by God (12:11–12). He says (facetiously) that the Corinthians should have boasted in *him*, since he was already superior to the "most eminent apostles" in whom they had put so much stock (even though these men regard him as a "nobody"). Yet, a "true apostle" must be able to prove his genuineness—not just with words or fancy speech, but with signs and miracles that accompany those whom God has genuinely sent (12:12; see Heb. 2:1–4). Miracles are the key ingredient for establishing credibility and divine approval; apart from these, no man can produce them by his own authority (John 10:37–38). Paul does not say that he could provide "signs and wonders and miracles" if necessary, but that he already *had* provided these—and the Corinthians were witnesses of them. And, instead of providing a single miracle of their own, the false teachers took advantage of the Corinthians and tried to turn them against a genuine apostle of Christ.

Paul had labored among the Corinthians longer than he did for most churches (a year and a half—Acts 18:11) and did not ask for compensation (1 Cor. 9:11–19). Despite such generosity, the Corinthians did not show much appreciation for Paul but gave their attention to those who took advantage of them and charged them for their services (12:13)! In response, Paul sarcastically apologizes that he did not do this as well ("Forgive me this wrong!"). If anything, the Corinthians should have defended Paul and his ministry, not chosen to side against him. They had no reason to regard him as "inferior" only because he had not "become a burden" to them financially. Their lack of gratitude toward Paul was compounded by the fact that they showed great respect to those who belittled him.

Questions

1.) Why was Paul "caught up to the third heaven," and yet not allowed to talk about what he saw or heard (12:2–4)? Is it unfair God expects us to "imitate" Paul (1 Cor. 11:1) but prevents us from seeing what He showed *him*? Please explain.

2.) Paul refers to his "thorn in the flesh" as a "messenger of Satan" (12:7). Might Satan afflict a Christian today with a 'thorn'? If so, how would he differentiate this "thorn" from any other typical adversity of life?

3.) "Power is perfected in weakness" (12:9). Can you think of at least five biblical examples where God has most certainly demonstrated this principle?
a)
b)
c)
d)
e)

4.) Why were the Corinthians indignant that Paul did not seek their payment for his services (12:13)? Yet, if he had asked for compensation, they may have accused him of preaching only for money. Money, however, is not the real issue here. What is the real issue, and why do you think Paul handled it the way he did?

Lesson Thirteen: Final Admonitions (12:14—13:10)

Paul Warns of Discipline (12:14-21): Instead of dealing with the Corinthians through written correspondence, Paul's intention is to stand before them in person (12:14). The "third time" (13:1) indicates two previous visits. Luke records one visit in Acts 18; biblical scholars consider the other to be an unrecorded so-called intermediate visit (see "Introduction"). He had intended to visit them earlier (recall comments on 1:15-17) but did not feel that it would have been productive at that time. Beyond this, we cannot know for certain what other visits Paul may have made to Corinth.

When he *does* come, he will continue his practice of not requiring them to compensate him for his services ("I will not be a burden to you"). As a father to his "children," Paul did not expect the Corinthians to pay for his expenses but sought to give *them* something instead. In a real sense, he gave himself: his time, effort, apostolic teaching, and spiritual counsel. "I do not seek what is yours, but you" is a telling statement: Paul is not after their material wealth, but is interested in their spiritual well-being—the health of their souls.

As he had done before (recall 6:11-13 and 7:2), Paul questions the Corinthians' lack of reciprocating love (12:15). Their respect and appreciation are what Paul naturally expects. However, this is not happening, and he draws attention to this glaring anomaly by assuming the voice of his accusers (12:16). He says, in effect, that while he did not charge them money for himself, he (being a "crafty fellow") deceived them over the collection for the saints in need (recall 8:1—9:15). Having been accused by the false teachers for taking that collection for himself, Paul presents this scenario before the Corinthians to evaluate. It is as if he says, "Given all that I have done for you and proved to you, does it *make sense* that I would now deceive you over money?"

Then there is the matter of Titus—a man of high character and excellent reputation—was he in on this alleged scam, too (Paul implicitly asks)? And what about the other notable men that accompanied Paul—are they part of a huge conspiracy meant to hoodwink the congregation (12:17–18)? In all this, Paul exposes the ridiculousness of the charges against him. First, there is no proof that these charges are true; second, the evidence takes us in the opposite direction; third, there are others involved besides Paul that must also be implicated (yet, without any proofs); and fourth, the accusers themselves lack character and credentials, undermining any sincerity to their charges.

Paul is not writing to the Corinthians simply to vindicate himself. Rather, he desires to build them up by proving the work of Christ in him for their benefit (12:19–21). When he arrives in Corinth (for his "third visit"), he wants this to be an edifying experience for both parties. Nonetheless, he is also prepared to render judgment and discipline (as an apostle of Christ) for those who stubbornly refuse to listen to him. In that case, neither he nor they may find each other in the way that they anticipated. He may find them still walking "according to the flesh" (recall 10:2); they may feel the severity of his power (recall 10:5–6). Some of the same problems Paul had encountered before—strife, jealousy, angry tempers, etc.—may still be present (see 1 Cor. 3:1–3).[105] If so, then he would be forced to take strong disciplinary action.

"God may humiliate me before you" (12:21)—i.e., instead of receiving honor for all the work he has done for this group of Christians, Paul may be humiliated instead by having to discipline them. Some of the very ones whom he has spent so much time and effort bringing to Christ may be those whom he will need to turn over to Satan (1 Cor. 5:5, 1 Tim. 1:20). He will need to confront those Corinthians who have persisted in their practice of "impurity, immorality, and sensuality." If they have not repented by the time of his visit, he will need to remove them from fellowship with the congregation (cf. Rev. 2:20–23).

Paul Promises a Third Visit (13:1–4): Whenever someone makes a charge against God's people, they must provide facts and not opinions or baseless hearsay (cf. 1 Tim. 5:19–20). And, to substantiate the charges, witnesses must be present (13:1).[106] In this case, the "witnesses" are Paul's own visits to the Corinthians: each visit has revealed the true nature of Paul's apostolic authority *and* the true nature of the Corinthians' response to that authority.

Not only this, but Paul has human witnesses as well—i.e., Titus and others who have accompanied him or have observed the situation for themselves and can testify accordingly. In effect, Paul is putting together a legal case against them to provide a full and complete investigation of the matter. While he does not desire a confrontation, he will do whatever is necessary to purify the Corinthian church—thus providing the "proof of the Christ who speaks in me" (13:2–3).

Paul's opponents accuse him of being weak and unimpressive (recall 10:10–11), but he will dispel these accusations when he confronts them face-to-face. Christ also appeared "weak" to His accusers yet proved Himself stronger than all of them. While Paul is "weak" as a human being in comparison to Christ, even so he is a chosen representative *of* Christ, and thus can assert himself when needed (13:4). Just as Christ has been exalted to everlasting life after undergoing the humiliation of being crucified as a mere Man, so Paul will live with Christ after undergoing the (sometimes) humiliating work of serving as His apostle. Meanwhile, the "power of God" can *save* people just as it can also *judge* them (recall 2:15–16): it serves as a two-edged sword.

"Test Yourselves" (13:5–10): The Corinthians have certainly "tested" Paul's authority as an apostle. Nonetheless, he has proven himself to be genuine and sincere through demonstrations of love, his integrity, his suffering for Christ, and the signs he had performed among them. Now he tells them to look in the mirror and examine *themselves* (13:5). In essence, he says, "I have proved my faithfulness to Christ; but what about you? Are *you* in the faith?" (Paul uses "the faith" here objectively, with reference to the Christian faith, as in 2 Tim. 4:7, Titus 1:13, Jude 1:3, etc.) Paul knows that some of the Corinthians have been deceived by the false teachers, but do *they* know this?

While Paul has already made investigation into the matter, they need to conduct their own investigation through the manner of self-examination (1 Cor. 11:28). What is at stake here is not merely who is right or wrong (as a matter of opinion) but who is genuinely acting like a *Christian* (as a matter of fellowship with God). This examination (or, proving) cannot use one's personal standard of approval (recall 10:12), but requires comparison to the revealed word of God. As for Paul and his companions, they have already been examined by God and have not failed the test (13:6; see 1 Cor. 4:2–4). This is evident through his teaching, conduct, and the miracles he has performed among them.

Paul is not wanting the Corinthians to fail but prays that they "do no wrong" (13:7). He is not trying to make *himself* look good by pointing out *their* faults. In fact, even if he and his companions are "unapproved," he still wants the Corinthians to do what is right. His goal is to proclaim and promote "the truth"—that is, *God's* truth, as revealed to him—and he has no right or intention to do otherwise (13:8–9a). His apostolic office is not for the purpose of changing, or even avoiding, the truth, but always in support of it. "Strong" and "weak" are relative terms, as measured against a fixed standard—in this case, the word of God.

If the Corinthians do what is right, they will be "made complete" (13:9b). This refers to an advanced measure of growth, maturity, experience, and discernment. All these things are what Paul seeks for the Corinthians since they have shown themselves to be lacking in them thus far (recall 12:20–21). His intention for writing them in advance is to give them time to examine themselves, address their problems, and repent of any sinful behavior (13:10) before he comes to them in person. He does not want to punish them ("use severity") but to praise them for their progress and improvement. Yet, the fact remains that Christ has commissioned him as His apostle not only to praise and edify ("building up") but also to reprove and punish ("tearing down"). It really depends upon the Corinthians themselves as to which actions Paul will take in dealing with them when he comes.

Questions

1.) Paul wrote that "children are not responsible to save up for their parents, but parents for their children" (12:14). Does this mean that the Corinthians were allowed to be irresponsible? Does it mean that parents today are to assume full responsibility for their children, regardless of what the children do (or refuse to do)? Does it mean that children today have no obligation to help their parents in any way? Or ... what?

2.) What is the purpose for having "two or three witnesses" confirm "every fact" (13:1)? (There is more than one answer.)

3.) How does one "test" and "examine" himself, as Paul instructed (13:5)? How could one "fail the test"—what exactly would be the cause of this failure?

4.) "Made complete" (13:9, 11) refers to achieving maturity or perfection (as in Mat. 5:48). Is being "made complete" something you do on your own, something God does *for* you, or a combination of both? Please support your answer with Scriptures, if possible.

Final Commendations and Closing Thoughts (13:11–14)

In these final verses (13:11–14), Paul winds up yet another long and difficult letter to the Corinthians. With that in mind, "finally" may mean more than just "at last" (13:11); it implies a "Let's not have to go through this again"—kind of sentiment. Paul has spent a tremendous amount of time, energy, and personal grief in dealing with these people. He is hopeful for a good outcome, but—at the time of his writing these words—it remains unclear as to what he will expect when he visits them again. We can only imagine the emotional turmoil he is enduring as he writes these words and wonders where all this is going.

Even so, Paul remains positive, optimistic, and cheerful. "Rejoice" can mean (here) "joy to you," "farewell" [KJV], or simply "good–bye" [NIV] (13:11). "Be made complete" also can mean "mend your ways," since the instruction refers to something the Corinthians are able to do for themselves.[107] God will bring them to spiritual completion but only if they *choose* to be complete and do what is necessary to that end. Paul's plea for completeness, like–mindedness, comfort, and peace is consistent with all his other epistles (1 Cor. 1:10, Phil. 1:27, 2:1–5, Col. 3:12–15, etc.). Paul's words in 13:12–13 are almost identical to the close of the previous letter (1 Cor. 16:20). The emphasis on "holy kiss" is not on the mode of greeting itself but its properness.[108] Just as Paul has proven to be genuine to the Corinthians, so they are to act genuinely toward one another. "The saints" here refers to the Macedonian Christians (probably the Philippians) with whom Paul is staying during the writing of this letter.

"Grace … love … fellowship" with the divine Personages of the triune Godhead (13:14) are promised to those who strive for the "oneness" for which Jesus prayed in John 17:20–23. This verse is one of the strongest in the NT for identifying these three Personages together, as well as showing the intimate union between them. The Father, Son, and Holy Spirit work in seamless cooperation toward the redemption of every soul that calls upon them for salvation; it is in the "name" (or, authority) of all three that each person becomes a Christian upon his baptism (Mat. 28:19).

- ❏ Through Christ, we are blessed with saving grace—the forgiveness of sins through His blood, as well as all the other blessings necessary for spiritual life (Eph. 1:3, 7).
- ❏ The love of God is what put His "eternal purpose" (Eph. 3:13) in motion and is the reason God sent Christ to be our Redeemer in the first place (John 3:16).
- ❏ Our "fellowship" involves a sharing, joint participation, or partnership with the Holy Spirit.[109] The Spirit sanctifies us (1 Pet. 1:3), intercedes for us (Rom. 8:26–27), and guides us (Gal. 5:16–17). As we submit to His leadership, we *walk* with Him in fellowship.

Anyone who has fellowship with any member of the Godhead necessarily has fellowship with the other two.

This has been a long, emotional, and difficult letter for Paul, yet he still expresses his strong desire for the spiritual welfare of these people. While his farewell comments here are unusually brief and direct, they still express a strong gesture of friendship and acceptance by him and the Lord, if the Corinthians persevere in the faith.

Sources Used for This Study

Barclay, William. *Letters to the Corinthians.* Louisville, KY: Westminster John Knox Press, 1975.

Barnes, Albert. *Barnes' Notes*, vol 11. Grand Rapids: Baker Book House Co., no date [orig. London: Blackie & Son, 1884].

Barrett, C. K. *The Second Epistle to the Corinthians.* Peabody, MA: Hendrickson Publishers, Inc., 1997.

Bruce, F. F. *The Book of the Acts.* Grand Rapids: Eerdman's Publishing, 1964.

Coffman, James Burton. *Commentary on 1 and 2 Corinthians.* Austin, TX: Firm Foundation, 1977.

_____. *Commentary on Acts.* Austin, TX: Firm Foundation, 1977.

Conybeare, W. J. and J. S. Howson. *The Life and Epistles of St. Paul.* Grand Rapids: Eerdman's Publishing Co., 1964.

Glaze, R. E. "Corinthians, Second Epistle to." *Holman's Illustrated Bible Dictionary* (electronic edition). Chad Brand, Charles Draper, and Archie England, eds. © 2003 by Holman Bible Publishers; database © 2014 by WORDsearch Corp.

Heading, John. *Second Epistle to the Corinthians.* Kilmarnock, Scotland: John Ritchie Ltd., 1966.

Hester, H. I. *The Heart of the New Testament.* Liberty, MO: The Quality Press, Inc., 1963.

Ironside, H. A. *Addresses on the Second Epistle to the Corinthians.* New York: Loizeaux Bros., 1954.

Jamieson, Robert, Andrew Fausset, and David Brown. *New Commentary on the Whole Bible: New Testament Volume* (electronic edition). Database © 2004 WORDsearch Corp.

Josephus: Complete Works, trans. William Whiston. Grand Rapids: Kregel Publications, 1978.

Kistemaker, Simon J. *New Testament Commentary: Exposition of the Second Epistle to the Corinthians.* Grand Rapids: Baker Book House Co., 1997.

Lenski, R. C. H. *Commentary on the New Testament: The Interpretation of St. Paul's First and Second Epistles to the Corinthians.* Peabody, MA: Hendrickson Publishers, Inc., 1998.

Lipscomb, David. *A Commentary on the New Testament Epistles: Second Corinthians and Galatians.* J. W. Shepherd, ed. Nashville: Gospel Advocate Co., 1979.

McGarvey, John William, and Philip Y. Pendleton. *The Standard Bible Commentary: Thessalonians, Corinthians, Galatians and Romans.* Cincinnati: Standard Publishing Foundation, 1916.

Robertson, A. T. *Word Pictures in the New Testament*, vol. 4. Grand Rapids: Baker Book House [no date].

Rupprecht, A. "Corinth." *Zondervan's Pictorial Encyclopedia*, vol. 1. Merrill C. Tenney, gen. ed. Grand Rapids: Regency Reference Library, 1976.

Strachan, R. H. *The Second Epistle of Paul to the Corinthians.* James Moffatt, ed. New York: Harper & Brothers Publishers, 1949.

Strong, James. *Strong's Talking Greek–Hebrew Dictionary* (electronic edition). Database © 2012 by WORDsearch Corp.

The International Standard Bible Encyclopedia. Geoffrey W. Bromiley, gen. ed. Grand Rapids: Eerdman's Publishing Co., 1939.

Vincent, Marvin R. *Vincent's Word Studies*, vol. 2 (electronic edition). Database © 2014 by WORDsearch Corp.

Vine, W. E. *Expository Dictionary of New Testament Words.* STBC [no date].

Endnotes

1	Simon J. Kistemaker, "Exposition of the Second Epistle to the Corinthians," *New Testament Commentary* (Grand Rapids: Baker Book House Co., 1997), 19.
2	H. I. Hester, *The Heart of the New Testament* (Liberty, MO: The Quality Press, Inc.1963), 302.
3	R. H. Strachan, "The Second Epistle of Paul to the Corinthians," *The Moffat New Testament Commentary* (New York: Harper & Brothers Publishers, 1949), xxix.
4	R. C. H. Lenski, "The Interpretation of St. Paul's First and Second Epistles to the Corinthians," *Commentary on the New Testament* (Peabody, MA: Hendrickson Publishers, Inc., 1998), 804.
5	An effort to dig a canal between the two bodies of water was long considered, even as far back as the time of Julius Caesar. No canal was completed, however, until French engineers constructed one in the late 19th century (Simon J. Kistemaker, *New Testament Commentary: 1 Corinthians* [Grand Rapids: Baker Books, 1993]), 3–4.
6	"Its wealth was derived from its commercial traffic by sea and by land, its pottery and brass industries, and its political importance as the capital of Achaia [Greece]. At its height it probably had a population of 200,000 free men and 500,000 slaves" (A. Rupprecht, "Corinth," *The Zondervan Pictorial Encyclopedia of the Bible, Vol. 1*, Merrill C. Tenney, gen. ed. [Grand Rapids: Regency Reference Library, 1976], 961).
7	"There were attached [to the temple of Aphrodite] 1,000 priestesses who were sacred prostitutes, and in the evenings they came down from the Acropolis and plied their trade on the streets of Corinth. ... Corinth became a synonym not only for wealth, luxury, drunkenness and debauchery, but also for filth" (William Barclay, *Letters to the Corinthians* [Louisville, KY: Westminster John Knox Press, 1975, 2002], 3; bracketed words are mine).
8	"The majority of the Corinthian Church had submitted to the injunctions of St. Paul, and testified the deepest repentance for the sins into which they had fallen. ... But there was still a minority, whose opposition seems to have been rather embittered than humbled by the submission which the great body of the Church had thus yielded. They proclaimed, in a louder and more contemptuous tone than ever, their accusations against the Apostle" (W. J. Conybeare and J. S. Howson, *The Life and Epistles of St. Paul*

[Grand Rapids: Eerdmans Publishing, 1964], 438).

9   J. W. McGarvey and Philip Y. Pendleton, *The Standard Bible Commentary: Thessalonians, Corinthians, Galatians and Romans* (Cincinnati: Standard Publishing Foundation, 1916), 167.

10   These Jews are not of the same mind as those whom Paul confronted in, say, Galatians. They are not imposing circumcision on Gentile believers; they do not insist on keeping the Law of Moses; etc.—things Paul has had to refute elsewhere. "[These] opponents were Jews, but Hellenistic [i.e., Greek–cultured] Jews, who imitated the style of propaganda used by the inspired figures of the Hellenistic world. 'In their behaviour [sic] and the style of their preaching they belong to that type of itinerant wandering prophets, magicians, and saviours [sic]…who gave themselves out to be God's envoys, and sought to exalt themselves by revelations and miracles' (Friedrich)" (C. K. Barrett, *Black's New Testament Commentary, vol. 8: The Second Epistle to the Corinthians* [Peabody, MA: Hendrickson Publishers, Inc., 1997], 28–29; bracketed words are mine).

11   McGarvey and Pendleton, *SBC*, 169.

12   "Comfort" is from the Greek *parakleseos*, related to *paraklete*, translated "Comforter" or "Helper" in John 14:16, 26, etc.; this latter word Jesus used to describe the (work of the) Holy Spirit (A. T. Robertson, *Word Pictures in the New Testament, Vol. IV* [Grand Rapids: Baker Books; no date], 208–209).

13   Lenski, *Interpretation*, 830.

14   On the other hand: "The Church's worst times are not times of suffering, of martyrdom. The Church's most dangerous periods are those when she is enjoying the patronage of the world. The Church is never in such grave danger as when the world is fawning upon it, when worldlings look upon it with favor" (H. A. Ironside, *Addresses on the Second Epistle to the Corinthians* [New York: Loizeaux Bros., 1954], 30).

15   Some manuscripts have *haploteti* (simplicity) instead of *hagioteti* (holiness); most of the commentators consulted favor this first usage: "in straightforwardness and godly sincerity … we have conducted ourselves …" (Kistemaker, *Exposition*, 54).

16   Lenski, *Interpretation*, 840–841.

17   "Vacillating" (NASB) is literally "fickleness" or "lightness (of sincerity)" or "levity" (versus seriousness) (W. E. Vine, *Expository Dictionary of New Testament Words* [STBC; no date], 92). Put another way: Paul was

not making a joke of the Corinthians by betraying their confidence in him.

18 "Anointed" [Greek, *chrisas*] is derived from *chrio*, from which we get "Christ" (Robertson, *Word Pictures*, vol. 4, 213). While we are not anointed in the same way as Christ, or for the same reason, we are anointed with the same Spirit (1 Cor. 12:13).

19 "The act [of our anointing] occurred in our baptism, as it did immediately after Christ's baptism [Mat. 3:16]. By means of His anointing Christ was placed into His high office and position; our anointing did the same for us. He was made King and Priest in the supreme sense, hence the supreme way in which God anointed Him; we were made kings and priests under Him, hence the way in which our anointing took place by means of baptism. Those who conceive of baptism as a mere sign and symbol must place the anointing elsewhere than in baptism, a thing that is most difficult to do" (Lenski, *Interpretation*, 854; bracketed words are mine).

20 Adapted from Strachan, *Second Epistle*, 59–60.

21 James Strong, *Strong's Talking Greek-Hebrew Dictionary*, electronic version (database © 2003 by WORDsearch Corp.), G728.

22 Some Bible scholars think that the next chapter ought to begin here, since there is an obvious transition in thought that flows seamlessly into chapter 2 (Albert Barnes, *Barnes' Notes, Vol. 11* [Grand Rapids: Baker Book House Co., no date], 24). Thus, this workbook uses 1:23 as the beginning of a new section rather than keeping 1:23–24 with the previous one.

23 R. E. Glaze, "2 Corinthians," *Holman's Illustrated Bible Dictionary*, electronic edition; Chad Brand, Charles Draper, and Archie England, eds. (© 2003 by Holman Bible Publishers; database © 2014 by WORDsearch Corp.).

24 This has been the dominant view for centuries. Some doubt this, however, and suggest that the man was a "stranger" to the Corinthian church—i.e., someone from outside of their group (Strachan, *Second Epistle*, 70; Barrett, *BNTC*, 89; etc.). However, such commentators offer no compelling evidence to deny what is the most natural conclusion.

25 This is also the conclusion of Kistemaker (*Exposition*, 78).

26 Lenski, *Interpretation*, 890; Lipscomb, *Commentary*, 39.

27 Conybeare and Howson, *Life and Epistles*, 444.

28 James B. Coffman, *Commentary on 1 and 2 Corinthians* (Austin, TX: Firm Foundation, 1977), 328. See also Marvin R. Vincent, *Vincent's Word Studies*, electronic edition (database © 2014 by WORDsearch Corp.), on 2:16.

"Paul uses the term of those who trade in the word of God, adulterating it for the purpose of gain or popularity."

29   There are two Greek words for "new" in the NT: *neos*, meaning "new in time," and *kainos*, meaning "new in time and quality." "It is the word *kainos* that both Jesus and Paul use of the new covenant, and the significance is that the new covenant is not only new in point in time; it is quite different in kind from the old covenant. It produces between human beings and God a relationship of a totally different kind" (Barclay, *Letters*, 225).

30   "The true sense of the Hebrew is given by the Septuagint: 'When he ceased speaking he put a veil on his face'; not because the Israelites could not endure the radiance, but that they should not see it fade away. Whenever Moses went into the presence of God he removed the veil, and his face was again illumined, and shone while he delivered God's message to the people. Then, after the delivery of the message, and during his ordinary association with the people, he kept his face covered" (Vincent, *Word Studies*, on 3:13).

31   "The Lord" in 3:17 must refer to its antecedent here in 3:16—technically, it refers to God in the citation quoted by Paul (Exod. 34:34). But Christ is Lord, and no man comes (or "turns") to the Father except through Him (John 14:6). Scholars wring their hands over whether "Lord" means God or Christ, yet in the end, it does not matter. Both are inextricably bound to the Holy Spirit and vice versa; a man cannot turn to one without turning to the other, since our fellowship is with both the Father and Son at once (1 John 1:3), as well as with the Holy Spirit (2 Cor. 13:14).

32   Adapted from Barnes, *Barnes' Notes*, 63.

33   Adapted from Barclay, *Letters*, 231–233.

34   "That Paul's Gospel has been rejected does not however prove that it is false" (Barrett, *BNTC*, 130).

35   "World," in this passage, is literally *aeon*, "a vast length of time but one that is marked by what transpires in it. Hence, 'this eon' is opposed to 'the eon about to come,' this world age in contrast to the coming blessed eternity" (Lenski, *Interpretation*, 960).

36   It should be noted that Paul regards Satan throughout this epistle as a real entity and not a fictitious bogeyman or theoretical concept (compare 2:11, 11:14, and 12:7).

37   Lipscomb, *Commentary*, 60. "Blinding, darkening, and hardening all refer to the same thing. The condition that results is sinful, and at the same time punishment for sin. Hardening occurs when the individual rebels

against God, who then allows Satan to have his way, with a result of further hardening.... Satan was never able to blind any person who had not already rebelled against God" (Coffman, *Commentary*, 347).

38   "We incidentally note that Paul reproduces the account of Moses [i.e., the Creation account in Genesis] as it is written: light was created by a fiat [or, authoritative declaration] in a timeless instant. And it is true, an evolution of light is unthinkable. Darkness cannot produce its absolute opposite; nor are stages in the coming into existence of light conceivable. The Scriptures testify that by His fiat God created light" (Lenski, *Interpretation*, 969; bracketed words are mine).

39   Robertson, *Word Pictures*, 225.

40   Strong, *Dictionary (electronic)*, G639.

41   The Greek word for "dying" here is *nekrosin*—not the usual word for death (*thanatos*)—which involves not only "death" itself but also the entire dying process (Kistemaker, *Exposition*, 149; Robertson, *Word Pictures*, 226). Thus, Paul implies not just the literal death of Jesus on the cross, but all the events, actions, and orchestrations that purposely led to His death.

42   Adapted from Lenski, *Interpretation*, 981-982.

43   Lipscomb, *Commentary*, 68.

44   "This is not metaphysics, but eschatology ...; the life to which Paul's observation leads is not one of abstraction, but of faith" (Barrett, *BNTC*, 148).

45   "[I]t is precisely bodilessness [sic] that makes this period of waiting undesirable in Paul's eyes. Already in this life we are waiting; we do not wish to do this in a bodiless state" (Barrett, *BNTC*, 154–155).

46   "God prepares the immortal covering while we are in the fleshly body serving Him, and becoming ready for the spiritual body from heaven. But if we be stripped of the mortal body before the spiritual body is ready, we shall be naked and in a ruined condition" (David Lipscomb, *A Commentary on the New Testament Epistles: Second Corinthians and Galatians*, J. W. Shepherd, ed. [Nashville: Gospel Advocate Co., 1979], 70).

47   Adapted by Vincent, *Word Studies (electronic)*, on 5:10.

48   "What a difference between a court on earth and the judgment seat in heaven! In human courts ..., the innocent are set free and the guilty serve terms of punishment and often must pay restitution. But no human court rewards a person according to deeds he or she has performed. By contrast, the divine Judge metes out rewards for good conduct and punishment for

unacceptable behavior" (Kistemaker, *Exposition*, 181).

49   Strong, *Dictionary (electronic)*, G1839. Festus also accused Paul of being "out of [his] mind" (Acts 26:24), because he was willing to put his convictions in the truth of the gospel ahead of his own well-being. "Real enthusiasts do not care if others think that they are fools. If people follow the Christian way of generosity, forgiveness and utter loyalty, there will always be worldly–wise people who will bluntly call them crazy" (Barclay, *Letters*, 247).

50   Paul seems to imply here: as Christ's death was intended to bring good to all men, so Paul's preaching (including his suffering for that preaching) is intended to do the same, regardless of how people view either Christ or Paul.

51   Strong, *Dictionary (electronic)*, G4243.

52   Robertson, *Word Pictures*, 233. The only other place this word is used in the NT is Eph. 6:20.

53   For a study on "grace" in the NT, I strongly recommend my book, *The Gospel of Saving Grace* (Spiritbuilding Publishers, 2020); go to www.spiritbuilding.com/chad.

54   The quote from Isa. 49:8 is in one of the "Servant songs" of Isaiah. These prophetic "songs" are messianic in nature, and thus anticipate the spiritual regeneration of Israel under God's Messiah (Christ). The gospel of Christ and the church age fulfill these "songs," and are appropriate to quote in the context of that fulfillment.

55   The principle here has already been put forward in the Law of Moses; see Lev. 19:19 and Deut. 22:10, for example. "The idea is that there are certain things which are fundamentally incompatible and which were never meant to be brought together" (Barclay, *Letters*, 262).

56   "Bound together" (or "unequally yoked"—see picture) implies a mismatched, discordant, and inappropriate union. An "unbeliever" is one who is not a Christian (as in 1 Cor. 6:6, 7:12, 10:27, 14:22, etc.), not a Christian who has fallen away from the faith. While many cite this verse to forbid marriages between believers and unbelievers, the actual context deals with joining in any alliance with non-Christians which forces the compromise of the believer's faith. This is what the Corinthians had done: they had enslaved themselves to false teachers and rejected Paul's apostolic authority. On the other hand, consider: "While I would not say that this passage is an absolute prohibition of the marriage of a believer to

an unbeliever, it certainly discourages it. … This passage certainly forbids persons so tying themselves to unbelievers in any business or any relation by which the believer is influenced or controlled by the unbeliever. How can a relationship be found that does this more effectually than the marriage relation?" (Lipscomb, *Commentary*, 93–94). Coffman is more direct: "This [passage] meant that no Christian had any business making alliances of any kind with pagans [i.e., unbelievers]; and yes, that certainly includes marriage. Why should any Christian wife accept a pagan for a husband?" (*Commentary*, 388–389; bracketed words added). In my own observation: it is very seldom that a believer who chooses to marry an unbeliever ever leads that person to Christ; far often, it is the unbeliever who leads the believer away from Christ, or, at the very least, brings all kinds of grief and torment to him (or her) (cf. 2 Pet. 2:7–8, in principle).

57   "Paul visualises [sic] a situation in which believer and unbeliever are rigidly fixed together in a common commitment, when this commitment is of a different kind to that allowed by God. Two may work together by necessity without being bonded together. This would be no yoke. But a yoke is formed by a definite agreement to share a life together, to share the organisational [sic] and financial running of a business together, to share interests together, to share religious experiences together, when a rigid yoke would mean a believer being irresistibly under the control of another partner" (John Heading, *Second Epistle to the Corinthians* [Kilamarnock, Scotland: John Ritchie Ltd., 1966], 117).

58   Barclay, *Letters*, 263.

59   This is hardly a new idea; see Isa. 52:11, Jer. 51:6, 9, and 45. It is also used in application to the destruction of "Babylon" (i.e., the Roman Empire) and the Christians' need to separate themselves from all the moral uncleanness of that depraved entity—i.e., to refuse the "mark" of its influence, control, and allegiance (Rev. 13:15–17, 14:9–10).

60   For example, consider Ittai's allegiance to David (2 Sam. 15:21), and what our own disposition ought to be (1 John 3:16).

61   Lipscomb, *Commentary*, 102.

62   Robertson, *Word Pictures*, 241.

63   Clearly, the "obedience of you all" is a general statement, not a literal one, since there remained in Corinth a group of people—we do not know how many—who challenged Paul's authority and belittled his apostleship. Chapters 10—13 will bear this out (Coffman, *Commentary*, 403–406).

64   "Wars, barbarian invasions, Roman settlement, and the restructuring of the province had contributed to a dismal financial status. ...Conversely, the city of Corinth flourished financially because of the volume of trade that its two harbors, Cenchrea and Lechaeum, generated. In brief, there was a distinct difference between Macedonia and Corinth in economic terms. Paul alludes to this contrast" (Kistemaker, *Exposition*, 273).

65   Barnes, *Barnes' Notes*, 178.

66   While it is often and traditionally taught (while taking up a collection from church members) that we are "commanded" to do this, Paul says just the opposite: "I am not speaking this as a command" (8:8, emphasis added). However, it is an expectation that we support the work of the church, and we did make this promise to God—and, necessarily, to our own congregation—when we came into Christ and identified as members of a specific group. Thus, we are not commanded to give, but we are expected to give, because we promised to do so when we identified with people—first, Christians everywhere; second, our own church family—who need our financial support.

67   To clarify: Paul is talking about actual, genuine, and pressing needs here, not normal circumstances. In other words, in times of one church's desperate need, other churches can and are expected to respond. "Need" is something God defines, in essence, through His word; it cannot be something that Christians decide arbitrarily or subjectively. However, Paul is not advocating that all the churches send money to one another until all of them have an equal amount.

68   Lipscomb, *Commentary*, 110; bracketed word is mine.

69   More has been said on this offering, and the means of collecting it, in my *1 Corinthians Commentary* (Spiritbuilding Publishers, 2024); go to www.spiritbuilding.com/chad.

70   William Ramsey has suggested that Luke and Titus are blood brothers, and that the "we" section (beginning in Acts 20:5) includes both men. Other commentators have found this to be a reasonable explanation as well (Kistemaker, Exposition, 293–294; F. F. Bruce, *The Book of the Acts* [Grand Rapids: Eerdmans, 1964], 406; James Coffman, *Commentary on Acts* [Austin: Firm Foundation, 1977], 383; and others).

71   The present tense of "I boast" leads us to believe that Paul is in Macedonia at the time of his writing, and that his boasting is something he is doing during the time he is writing to the Corinthians (Robert Jamieson,

Andrew Fausset, and David Brown, *New Commentary on the Whole Bible: New Testament Volume*, electronic edition [database © 2004 WORDsearch Corp.], "Introduction to 2 Corinthians").

72   As a parallel to this, consider the procrastination of the priests when King Jehoash wanted to collect money for the repair of the temple in 2 Kings 12:4–7.

73   Barnes, *Barnes' Notes,* 196; Strong, *Dictionary (electronic),* G2129.

74   "Bountifully" and "sparingly" are relative terms here. We should not measure the specific dollar amount of one's contribution against another's but should instead focus upon the quantity of one's contribution in proportion to what he can give. A common citation here is that of the rich Jews who "gave" out of their surplus, contrasted with the poor widow who gave a few copper coins—yet her contribution was proportionately far greater than theirs; see Mark 12:41–44, Luke 21:1–4. Theirs was not a true sacrifice, but hers was.

75   This is put forward as a general principle. We should not assume that giving a large sum of money to the church will be rewarded by God with an even larger sum of money. How you give to God is yours to determine; how God repays you is His to determine. He may bless one who gives a large financial contribution with a gift that has nothing to do with money (or vice versa). The ultimate gifts we receive are those which are found in Christ ("every spiritual blessing"—Eph. 1:3), which cannot be received unless one's heart is already humble, merciful, and generous toward God's people ("rich in good works"—1 Tim. 6:18).

76   Paul's statement here (9:7a) needs to be paired with what he already said earlier—"as he may prosper" (1 Cor. 16:2). One's heart may be very generous, but he must be realistic about what he should give. If his prosperity is limited, then so will his giving be—not because he is not generous, but because his income is small. On the other hand, if his prosperity is great but his giving is small, then he is one who has "[closed] his heart against" his fellow believers and the work of the church (1 John 3:17). The two things—purpose of heart and the level of one's prosperity—are related. One cannot give more than he has, nor is he expected to do so (recall 8:12).

77   The Greek word here is *hilaros,* from which we get our English word "hilarious" (Robertson, *Word Pictures,* 248). This is the only occasion in which this Greek word is used in the NT. Obviously, the usage of this word

has changed somewhat since Paul's day, since God does not love a "hilarious" giver, but one who joyfully and gladly releases his gifts to those in need of them.

78   "Service" is from *leitourgias*, "public work"; thus, "public service either in worship to God (Luke 1:23) or benefaction to others (2 Cor. 9:12, Phil. 2:30). Our word liturgy is this word" (Robertson, *Word Pictures,* 249).

79   "It is perfectly correct to say that chapters 1 to 9 are 'we' chapters, and that these last are 'I' chapters" (Lenski, *Interpretation,* 1196; see also Barrett, *BNTC,* 244). The tone of this last major section of the epistle concerns Paul specifically, and answers the charges and allegations made against him personally; other men (like Titus in 12:18) are mentioned only incidentally.

80   Barnes, *Barnes' Notes,* 208.

81   Ibid., 212; Strong, *Dictionary (electronic),* G772.

82   McGarvey and Pendleton, *SBC,* 223. "What they failed to understand was that measurement by their own standards meant in effect the use of no standards at all" (Barrett, *BNTC,* 263).

83   "In the oriental culture of that day, an engagement was equivalent to marriage without consummation. The betrothal period lasted for one year, during which the bride and bridegroom prepared for the wedding ceremony. From the day of her betrothal, the woman legally was the wife of her future husband but she remained a virgin until the wedding day. In addition, the engagement might not be broken. If this happened, it was considered a divorce. … The bride had to remain a pure virgin to be presented to her husband. So Paul exerts himself to keep the church pure from doctrine contrary to the gospel as he strives to present her to Christ" (Kistemaker, *Exposition,* 359).

84   "The account of the temptation as recorded in Genesis is regarded by the inspired writers of the New Testament not as a myth, or an allegory, or fiction, but a true story" (Lipscomb, *Commentary,* 138).

85   Kistemaker, *Exposition,* 363.

86   "Unskilled" is from the Greek word *idiotes* (from which we get our word "idiot"), which referred in Paul's day to someone with no technical training—in essence, a layman or laywoman (Barclay, *Letters,* 292). In my opinion, Paul speaks ironically here, not literally. His speeches recorded in Acts, for example, do not reveal an amateur speaker, but a polished and well-trained orator—not with all the frills and eloquent phrases one

would expect from a professional Grecian orator but a solid and convincing speaker, nonetheless. The Athenians in Greece, for example, would not have invited an amateur speaker to address them at their celebrated rostrum (Acts 17:19ff). Even the Lycaonians viewed him as the chief speaker of the gods (Acts 14:12). Paul's addresses before the Jews, Roman governors, and even a room packed with Roman officials (Acts 25:23), show him to be fully capable of providing an intelligent and influential argument, regardless of the style or charisma that one was expecting otherwise.

87   The word "rob" comes from an old Greek word [*sylao*] which refers to a conqueror stripping a slain foe of his weapons on the battlefield (Kistemaker, *Exposition*, 369).

88   McGarvey and Pendleton, *SBC*, 229.

89   Whether "hits you in the face" refers to insulting behavior or actual striking in the face (as in John 18:22 or Acts 23:2) is not known, but in either case it is a demeaning and very unchristian action, which is Paul's point.

90   JFB, *Commentary (electronic)*, on 11:23.

91   Lipscomb, *Commentary*, 150.

92   Paul has done this on several other occasions: Rom. 1:9, 9:1, 2 Cor. 1:23, Gal. 1:20, and 1 Tim. 2:7.

93   King Aretas reigned over Nabatea, an Arabian kingdom, from 9 BC to AD 40. During the reign of Caligula (37–41), he exercised authority over Damascus, which concurs with Paul's time-frame and account; this places Paul's conversion at approx. AD 34. Incidentally, Aretas was the father-in-law of Herod Antipas, until Herod divorced the king's daughter to marry his brother Philip's wife (Mark 6:17–18) (Josephus, *Complete Works* [Grand Rapids: Kregal Publications, 1978], *Antiquities*, 18.5.1, 3; H. E. Dosker, "Aretas," *ISBE* [© 1979 Wm. B. Eerdmans Publishing Co.; database © 2013 by WORDsearch Corp]). Luke (in Acts 9:23–25) emphasizes that Paul was escaping a plot of the Jews, while Paul points to the real source of the antagonism, which was King Aretas himself. No doubt both parties (the Jews and the king) were in collusion.

94   "The whole passage is most perplexing, from the obscurity of its connection with what precedes and what follows. Why did St. Paul mention his escape from Damascus in so much detail? Was it merely as an event ignominious [lit., humiliating or embarrassing] to himself? This seems to be the best view, but it is far from satisfactory" (Conybeare and Howson, *Life and Epistles*, 461; bracketed words are mine).

95   "These men [Judaizers] also laid stress on 'visions and revelations' … Otherwise Paul's words … about his own visions are irrelevant to the situation" (Strachan, *Second Epistle,* xxv; bracketed word is mine).

96   "There is a difference between the two words vision and revelation. [A vision] is the means that God sometimes used to communicate with men. … [A revelation] is an unfolding, an uncovering of what had previously been hidden. … Thus revelation concerns the knowledge of divine Persons, and of doctrinal truth. Revelation is given for the heart and for faith, while visions are given for the mind and for works" (Heading, *Second Epistle,* 215–216; all emphases are his; bracketed words are mine).

97   The "fourteen years" here has no connection to the "fourteen years" mentioned in Gal. 2:1. However, "fourteen," as a double-seven number, likely does have some sacred significance, as does the number seven by itself; see Mat. 1:17, for example.

98   Vincent, *Word Studies* (electronic), on Luke 23:43. The symbolic connection between the physical Garden of Eden and the spiritual Paradise of God is unavoidable.

99   "The Greek has the term *skolops*, which means either a stake or a thorn. It will not do to think of impalement or crucifixion, because Paul always uses *stauros* when he writes about the cross. Here the word means a thorn or some other object that pierces Paul's flesh and injures him. … Most scholars agree that this term must be interpreted literally. That is, Paul endured physical pain" (Kistemaker, *Exposition,* 415).

100   "Torment" [KJV, "buffet"] comes from a Greek word (*kolaphizei*) which means "to strike with the [closed] fist so that the hard knuckles make the blow sting and crush" (Lenski, *Interpretation,* 1300; bracketed words are mine); it is used also in Mat. 26:27 and 1 Cor. 4:11.

101   In the Greek text, "sufficient" is the first word out of the Lord's mouth: "Sufficient is My grace for you …" This emphasizes the Lord's answer: the answer is not merely "grace," but the sufficiency of grace.

102   For a thorough study of the subject of grace, I strongly recommend my book, *The Gospel of Saving Grace* (Spiritbuilding Publishers, 2020); go to www.spiritbuilding.com/chad.

103   Literally, "For My power is brought to its finish [or, completion; perfection] in weakness" (Lenski, *Interpretation,* 1304; bracketed words are mine). "Power is continually increased as the weakness grows. … The human weakness opens the way for more of Christ's power and grace" (Robertson, *Word Pictures,* 266).

104   Strong, *Dictionary (electronic)*, G1981. This is the only time this compound Greek word [*episkenoo*] is used in the NT.

105   The worldliness that Paul describes (in 12:20) is common to every group of Christians (in any given congregation) that resists sound doctrine and biblical leadership. These behaviors manifest an ugly and non-spiritual attitude toward God and His people and contradict everything we know about Christ and the Holy Spirit's influence among believers (Phil. 2:1–5, Gal. 5:19–23). Those who exhibit such behaviors interfere with the preaching, shepherding, and growth of their own congregation; they are, in effect, the saboteurs of church work everywhere.

106   A "witness" is not always an eyewitness—a first-hand observer of "what happened"—but can be someone who testifies to the accuracy and inescapable conclusions of the facts. And a witness can even be an inanimate object—say, "heaven and earth" (Deut. 4:26 and 30:19)—if the facts are so clear and unavoidable to make them irrefutable.

107   Kistemaker, *Exposition*, 457; Barrett, BNTC, 342.

108   "I think, beyond all doubt, that the object of the Holy Spirit in referring to the kiss was to regulate a social custom, and not to institute an ordinance. It was customary to greet with a kiss, and the Holy Spirit said it should be a holy one" (Lipscomb, *Commentary*, 174). Coffman quotes Clement of Alexandria, who says: "Love is not proved by a kiss. … There are those that make the church resound with a kiss, not having love itself within. The shameless use of a kiss occasions foul suspicions and evil reports. … Gentle manners require that a kiss be chaste and with a closed mouth. There is an unholy kiss, full of poison, counterfeiting sanctity. 'This is the love of God,' says John, 'That we keep his commandments,' not that we stroke each other on the mouth" (Coffman, *Commentary*, 504).

109   The Greek word here [*koinonia*] is related to our word "communion"; Strong, *Dictionary (electronic)*, G2842.

www.ingramcontent.com/pod-product-compliance
Lightning Source LLC
Chambersburg PA
CBHW040322050426
42453CB00017B/2433